CANDLE MAGIC
for Beginners

Richard Webster is the author of twenty-eight books published by Llewellyn during the past decade, as well as many others published in New Zealand and elsewhere. A resident of New Zealand, he travels extensively, giving workshops, seminars, and lectures on the topics of which he writes.

CANDLE MAGIC for BEGINNERS

The Simplest Magic You Can Do

Richard Webster

2004
Llewellyn Publications
St. Paul, Minnesota 55164-0383, U.S.A.

First Edition
First Printing, 2004

Cover design by Lisa Novak
Cover photograph © Hannah Lynch Photography
Editing and interior design by Connie Hill
Interior art by Llewellyn Art Department

Library of Congress Cataloging-in-Publication Data
Webster, Richard.
    Candle magic for beginners : the simplest magic you can do / Richard Webster — 1st ed.
        p.   cm.
    Includes bibliographical references and index.
    ISBN 0-7387-0535-7
    1. Magic. 2. Candles and lights. I. Title.
BF1623.C26W43   2004   2004048419
133.4'3—dc22

Llewellyn Worldwide does not participate in, endorse, or have any authority or responsibility concerning private business transactions between our authors and the public.

All mail addressed to the author is forwarded, but the publisher cannot, unless specifically instructed by the author, give out an address or phone number.

Any Internet references contained in this work are current at publication time, but the publisher cannot guarantee that a specific location will continue to be maintained. Please refer to the publisher's website for links to authors' websites and other sources.

Llewellyn Publications
A Division of Llewellyn Worldwide, Ltd.
P.O. Box 64383, Dept. 0-7387-0535-7
St. Paul, MN 55164-0383, U.S.A.
www.llewellyn.com

Printed in the United States of America

Dedication

For my good friends
Erskine and Charlotte Payton

Also by Richard Webster

Contents

Introduction

My introduction to candle magic came when I was sixteen years old. I told a school friend about a problem I had, and received an unexpected reply. He suggested I burn some candles. His mother regularly used candle magic, and he had picked up the basics of the art. He guided me through a short ritual, and despite my skepticism, my problem disappeared. I was still not totally convinced that burning candles had resolved the situation, but I became intrigued and have been exploring the subject ever since. Over the years I have used candle magic to help me with a variety of difficulties, and many goals. I have benefited enormously from candle magic, even if on occasions the aid came in unexpected ways.

It is not surprising that candle magic is so popular, as there is something special about lighting a candle and watching it burn. People have always been fascinated with fire, and all around the world have used flame as an accompaniment to prayer and magic for thousands of years. Primitive people danced and sang around fires to invoke the spirits. Even today, Christianity, Judaism, and Hinduism still associate fire with divinity.

Before candles were invented, people used small oil lamps, called votive lamps, when making prayers and offerings to the gods. Beeswax candles were used in Egypt and Crete from about 3000 BCE, and helped people send their prayers to God.[1] Depictions of cone-shaped candles on saucers can be found on the walls of tombs in Thebes. The ancient Romans used candles and tapers made of wax and tallow.

It is believed that King Alfred the Great (CE 849–899) used candles to measure time. He had candles made that burned for exactly four hours, when placed in a special horn-shaped lantern that protected them from being extinguished by a draft.[2]

Guilds were set up in the thirteenth century, and candlemakers sold their wares door to door. Seventy-one candlemakers were listed in a Paris tax list in 1292.[3] Because wax candles were expensive in the Middle Ages, they were usually found only in monasteries, churches, and the homes of the wealthy.[4] Poorer people had to make do with foul-smelling rushlight candles, made by dipping rushes into leftover cooking fat.

In colonial times in America, housewives made candles in the fall. Rods, containing a row of wicks, were repeatedly dipped into a kettle full of boiling water and molten tallow until the candles reached the desired thickness. This task would take a full day.

Until the nineteenth century, people were limited to beeswax and tallow candles. However, as the century progressed an enormous number of improvements were developed. In 1811, French chemist Michel-Eugène Chevreul discovered the stearine process when he separated the fatty acid from the glycerin of tallow. This enabled the production of vastly superior candles of stearic acid. These candles were harder than the old tallow ones, and burned for much longer. They also burned more brightly.

Candlemakers found that spermaceti, taken from the sperm whale, made excellent candles that produced an extremely bright light, but these are no longer made as whales are protected animals. In 1850, Dr. James Young patented a process that extracted paraffin wax from crude oil. Paraffin candles were cheaper than spermaceti or beeswax candles, and produced just as much light. Paraffin candles are still being made today.

Another major nineteenth-century development was the invention of candle-molding machinery that enabled manufacturers to produce candles more efficiently and cheaply than before. This meant that even the poorest people could afford to buy them.

Today, of course, candles are used mainly for decorative and celebratory purposes. Candlemaking is a popular hobby, and there is an increasing interest in the age-old subject of candle magic.

Not surprisingly, there is much folklore connected with candles. Probably the most important of these concerns the symbolism behind blowing out the candles on a birthday cake. In this ritual the emphasis is taken off the candles and all the attention is focused on the breath. This means that the breath (life) continues beyond all the years indicated by the candles.

Candlemas commemorates the purification of Mary that occurred when she took her young son, Jesus, to the temple and was told that he would become the Light to the World. February 2 is forty days after Christmas, the time allotted in Jewish law for a woman to be considered cleansed after giving birth to a son. Consequently, Candlemas signifies cleansing and purification, as well as the return of light after the darkness of winter. The Christian Candlemas is derived from an earlier Roman ritual in which women carried candles to honor Juno Februata, the virgin mother of Mars, on February 2. This ritual symbolizes new life, and promises the return of spring and all that season implies for everyone's wellbeing. Christians chose this day for Candlemas deliberately. Pope Sergius renamed the day to "undo this foul use and custome, and turn it onto God's worship and our Lady's."[5]

The Feast Day of Saint Brigid, the Celtic goddess, happens to be celebrated on February 1 or 2, as is Imbolg, one of the four witches' Sabbaths. (The others are Roodmas on April 30 [alternatively observed as Beltane, on May 1],

Lammas on August 1, and Samhain, or Halloween, on October 31.) Candles play a part in each of these celebrations.

The light of a candle has always been considered a sign of spiritual illumination, compared to the darkness that symbolizes ignorance. Consequently, in the Christian tradition, a candle can represent Christ, faith, and witness. Candles are used a great deal in the Catholic Church as symbols of light and faith.

The candle can also be considered a metaphor for the brief time we spend in this lifetime, and how easily life can be extinguished. In religious paintings a candle often symbolizes the human soul.

It used to be thought that when a candle blew out during a religious service it was a sign that evil spirits were not far away. Evil spirits prefer darkness to light, and candles played an important role in keeping them at a distance. Candles used to be lit at the birth of a child to keep evil spirits away. They were also lit when someone was dying to prevent evil spirits from seizing the person's soul.

In the north of England, candles are still sometimes used as a love charm. In one such charm, two pins are stuck into a candle; the belief is that the person's love will arrive by the time the candle has burned down to the pins.

During the Jewish Festival of Lights (Hanukkah), one candle is burned on the first night, two on the second, three on the third, and so on until the eighth night. The candles signify that the Jewish faith is inextinguishable and ever-growing. Hanukkah is an important Jewish observance commemorating the rededication of the Second Temple of Solomon in Jerusalem in 165 BCE. It had been destroyed three years earlier by the Syrian king, Antiochus IV Epiphanes, who had tried to destroy the Jewish religion.

A Jewish tradition that was popular in medieval times was to light a candle ten days before Yom Kippur, the Day of Atonement. This was the time when God decided everyone's fate for the next twelve months. If the candle went out, it was a sign that the person would not live long enough to see the next Day of Atonement. If it burned completely, it meant the person would live for at least another year.

Bees were considered messengers to the gods, and beeswax candles were used in churches because of their close connection with heaven.

The hypnotic fascination that the candle flame produces gives a clue as to why people began burning candles for magical purposes. The flickering flame appears to ignite something deep inside us that connects us with the infinite, and with all humanity. Life, death, and rebirth are all revealed by a candle. The relationship between the human soul and a solitary candle burning in the dark reminds people of the power of the human spirit, and how it can turn darkness into light. How you can use candles to achieve your goals and turn darkness into light is the purpose of this book.

One
What Is Candle Magic?

According to the *Unabridged Random House Dictionary of the English Language*, magic is the art of achieving a desired result by the use of certain mysterious techniques, such as incantations or ceremonies. Aleister Crowley, the famous twentieth-century magician, defined magic as "the Science and Art of causing Change to occur in conformity with Will."[1] One of my favorite definitions of magic comes from Florence Farr, a leading member of the Golden Dawn: "Magic consists of removing the limitations from what we think are the earthly and spiritual laws that bind or compel us. We can be anything because we are All."[2] I particularly like the phrase "we can be anything," as magic

1

allows us to overcome apparently insurmountable obstacles and attract to us whatever it is we want.

There are many forms of magic, some of them extremely difficult to master. Candle magic has a huge advantage over virtually all other forms of magic as it is straightforward and uncomplicated. You do not have to remember the 365 names of God, for instance. At its most basic, you can light a candle and make a wish. Of course, there is a lot more to it than that, and the rituals need to be performed properly to be effective. Nevertheless, candle magic stands alone among the magical arts for its ease and effectiveness.

Here are just some of the advantages that candle magic has over other forms of magic:

- The rituals are simple, but effective
- The costs are minimal, and the props can be made or bought anywhere
- There is no need for special robes or intricate ceremonies
- The rituals can be performed anywhere, indoors or out
- There is no need for years of training; you can start right away, and experience results immediately
- Candle magic is extremely versatile; rituals can be used to attract, to repel, to protect, and to divine the future

You might be surprised to learn that you have been practicing candle magic since you were a toddler. Making a wish when you blew out the candles on your birthday cake is a good example of candle magic. First of all you concentrated, and then you made a wish. Your subconscious mind received this request and made the wish happen.

Many people perform candle magic unconsciously. A good friend of mine lights candles every Sunday night while writing in her journal. This is a special, quiet time for her, and she looks forward to it all week long. She has a large selection of candles and chooses the ones that appeal to her at the time. Somehow, even though she knows nothing about the subject, she always chooses the candles that relate to what is going on in her life at the time.

Our former next-door-neighbors used to burn a beeswax candle in their bedroom for an hour or two every night before going to bed. They believed that it helped them sleep better, and also made them more likely to remember helpful dreams. Interestingly, my friends at Pheylonian Beeswax Candles in Canada told me that beeswax candles produce negative ions that help create a balanced environment.[3] Consequently, at the same time that my neighbors thought they were performing a form of candle magic, their candles were busy creating a more harmonious and sweeter environment. No wonder they slept so well.

I have been guilty of lighting candles for a specific purpose while entertaining people. If they had thought about it, my guests would have assumed that I was using the candles for atmosphere and decoration, rather than for a magical purpose.

Candles are incredibly comforting, even when used simply to decorate a dining table. There is something about the romantic atmosphere they create that makes them seem magical and uplifting. Candles create warmth, light, and feelings of brightness and joy. When you gaze into a flame it is easy to see how candle magic began.

The Roman Catholic, Greek Orthodox, and Russian Orthodox churches all burn candles when making requests. Pagans also burn candles for the same reasons. Candle magic has been used by people of all religions, and of no religion, to effect change and to make their wishes come true.

Burning candles is one thing; burning them to attain a desired result is another. Candles that are burned with a specific aim in mind become powerful tools that enable you to perform real magic. This is because the person making the request concentrates on the desired result, which subconsciously impresses this desire into the candle. As the candle burns, the request is sent out into the universe where it is manifested. The candle is, in effect, the link between the mind of the person making the request and the Universal Mind, whoever or whatever you perceive that as being. The Universal Mind is spiritual in nature. The candle is solid matter that is transmuted into spirit as it burns. This, coupled with intent, creates incredibly powerful magic.

It is interesting to note that all four elements are always involved in candle magic. An unlit candle represents the element of Earth. However, when it is placed in contact with Fire, the candle starts to melt, creating liquid wax (symbolizing Water) and smoke (Air). The Rosicrucians were referred to as the "fire-philosophers." They used fire to symbolize transmutation, because when a candle is burned it creates light.[4]

It goes without saying that candle magic should be used only for good. Karma follows the law of cause and effect. Any good deeds you do build up a store of good, or positive, karma. Any bad deeds build up bad, or negative, karma that will have to be repaid sooner or later. Consequently, it is vitally important that you perform any form of magic with pure motives. Your magic must harm no one.

Candle magic involves a number of factors:

- You must have an aim, desire, or need in mind; you need to remain focused on your goal while performing all of these steps

- As in all types of magic, there needs to be an emotional involvement

- You have to choose the correct candle, or candles

- You must dress the candle

- You must consecrate the candle

- You must burn the candle; this is usually done in the form of a ritual that helps send the desired energies out into the universe

- You need to believe in the power of your magic, and wait expectantly for the desired result

- Naturally, you can not expect the candle ritual to do everything for you; you need to do whatever else is required to make your desire a reality; this usually entails work; if your spell involves finding a new partner, for instance, you have to do your part by going to places where you are likely to meet him or her—creating a spell and then staying at home will not work

We will be covering all of these factors in the following chapters. To begin, though, we need to look at the items that are required to perform candle magic. That is the subject of the next chapter.

Two

Candles and Other Implements

Obviously, you will need at least one candle to perform candle magic. There are many types to choose from, and, most of the time, your personal preference is the most important factor. Over the years, I have performed candle magic with a large number of different types of candles.

One of the most successful experiences I have had with candle magic used a candle in the shape of a popular cartoon character. We were staying in a rented cottage for our summer vacation at the time, and this was the only candle in the house. I was a bit doubtful about using it, but the results far surpassed my expectations. This experience taught me that any candle will work, as long as the intent and desire are strong enough.

Candle Types

There are two materials most commonly used in the making of candles:

Beeswax Candles

Beeswax candles are made by rolling a sheet of beeswax around a candle wick. When burned these candles produce a halo-like effect that looks like a golden glow around the flame. This is actually a ball of heat, because beeswax candles burn much hotter than paraffin candles. Many people prefer using beeswax candles to other types because beeswax is a natural, pure fuel, and produces beneficial negative ions. These candles also have a pleasing natural odor.

Paraffin Candles

Most of the candles available today are made from paraffin wax. Paraffin wax, made from the residue of petroleum, can be bleached white and then dyed in different colors. Scent is frequently added, also.

Candles for Special Purposes

Three main types of candles can be used in candle magic: altar, astral, and offertory candles. In addition, a variety of other candles are available that will suit your purposes.

Altar Candles

Altar candles are not essential to candle magic, but are commonly used because they symbolize the deities or universal energies with which you are communicating. They can be any size or shape, but are usually tall and slender. They are generally taller than the other candles in the ritual, and are almost always white in color. Altar candles are placed on either side of the altar, and should be placed in position with a degree of reverence as they depict the forces you are contacting. The altar candle to your right when facing your altar depicts male energies, and the candle to your left symbolizes female energies. Altar candles are lit first and extinguished last when performing candle magic.

Archangel Candles

Archangel candles are burned to gain protection from the archangels. A blue or gold candle represents Michael, and this candle is burned to provide protection from physical, mental, emotional, or psychic attacks. Green or pink symbolizes Raphael, and this candle is burned to provide healing energies to the body, mind and spirit. Indigo or white symbolizes Gabriel, and this candle is burned to gain guidance and wisdom. Gold or purple symbolizes Uriel, and this candle is burned to gain peace, tranquillity, and freedom from fear.

Astral Candles

Astral candles symbolize the people involved in the spell or ritual. Naturally, one of these candles will represent you, while other astral candles can represent the other people involved. Astral candles vary in color, depending on the horoscope sign, or other details, of the person they represent. Someone born under the sign of Aries, for instance, would be represented by a red candle. If you do not know the person's horoscope sign, you can use either a white candle or a candle of any color that seems right to you to represent this person. Astral candles selected by someone's horoscope sign are also known as zodiac candles.

Cat Candles

White candles shaped like a cat are burned to protect pregnant women. They are also burned to help make wishes become a reality. Black cat candles are burned to increase the energy and potency of any magic spell.

Cross Candles

Cross candles are crucifix-shaped, and are generally burned to provide protection. They are also frequently used as altar candles. Cross candles can be used to symbolize protective angels that protect your home and family. One candle is burned every day for a week, and the color of the candle is determined by the day of the week:

Monday: White
Tuesday: Red
Wednesday: Orange
Thursday: Blue

Friday: Green
Saturday: Black
Sunday: Yellow

Knob Candles

Knob candles are made from seven balls of wax, one on top of the other, with a single wick. One knob is burned each day for seven days, while the person burning the candle thinks about his or her goal. These are sometimes known as wish candles. Knob candles can be obtained in any color, depending on your specific goal. By far the most popular color is white. White knob candles are burned to provide protection for you and your loved ones.

Lunar Candles

Lunar candles are usually moon-shaped. However, any candle with a moon depicted on it can be called a lunar candle. They are burned to increase the power of moon magic, and for anything to do with Goddess rituals.

Novena Candles

Novena candles can be purchased at religious supply stores. These are cylindrical candles, enclosed in heat-resistant glass, and they burn for seven days. Some of these candles are made to burn for twelve days, but the seven-day candle is much more common. A plain novena candle contains no markings. These are the better choice to use for candle magic. A spiritual novena candle usually has pictures of saints and other holy people on the front of the glass container. Prayers and psalms are often printed on the back. You will occasionally come across specialty novena candles. These candles are burned for a specific purpose that is depicted on the glass container.

Offertory Candles

Offertory candles symbolize whatever it is you are seeking in the ritual. A number of these can be used in a single spell. The colors of offertory candles relate to the purpose they are being used for. An orange candle, for instance, symbolizes attraction, while a green candle represents money. If the purpose of your spell is to attract money, you would use two offertory candles, one orange, and the other green.

Passing Over Candles

A passing over candle is burned for three days when someone dies, and can help the person make the transition to the other world. It is also believed to provide peace and help to the loved ones left behind. Passing over candles date back to the ancient Hebrews who used candles to protect the dying. Candles were also burned for a week after the person's death.[1] In modern-day Ireland, twelve candles are often placed around the coffin to protect the deceased from evil. Incidentally, it is considered bad luck in Ireland to burn three candles in a room, because three candles are traditionally burned at Irish wakes.

Phallus Candles

Phallus candles are penis-shaped and are burned to provide help for anything to do with male sexuality, such as premature ejaculation or impotence. They are also burned in fertility and sex magic rites. (The female equivalent is the yoni candle.)

Protection Candles

Protection candles are used to protect you when you are performing any form of destructive magic, such as banishing an illness. They are usually white, and can be of any size and shape. Some novena candles can be used as protection candles, especially if the depiction on the glass is of one of the saints.

Skull Candles

Skull candles are shaped like a human skull, and are burned when it is necessary to get inside someone's head to inspire change. Green skull candles enhance memory retention, and also aid people with mental problems. Red skull candles can be burned to encourage someone to lose interest in you. White skull candles are useful in healing, as they send pleasant thoughts of good health and well being to people who are ill.

Skull candles can also represent bureaucracy. If you are having problems with local government, for instance, you can burn a skull candle of the correct color to encourage them to consider your interests.

Vigil Candles

A vigil candle is burned for several days, or even weeks, to provide help and assistance to anyone who needs it. A vigil candle can be of great help to someone who has been close to death and is recovering from an illness. Once the candle has been completely burned, it is replaced with a fresh one.

Yoni Candles

Yoni candles are vulva-shaped and are burned to help anything to do with female sexuality, such as childbirth. They are also used in fertility and sex magic rites. (The male equivalent is the phallus candle.)

Candle Maintenance

You are unlikely to have many problems if you buy good quality candles. However, odd things may occur from time to time.

Remember that candles tend to smoke more in a small room. This is because candles need to breathe. You must consider this when choosing the right place for candle magic. Scented candles smoke more than unscented ones—something you should bear in mind when buying candles.

If a candle is smoking more than it should, put it out and allow it to cool. Then trim the wick to about one-quarter inch. Most of the time, this will solve the problem. You should never attempt to trim the wick while the candle is burning. Check for any extraneous substances in the molten wax around the wick, also, in case that is the cause of the excess smoke.

Make sure that your candles are placed firmly upright in their holders to avoid wax dripping onto your altar. Drafts can also cause candles to drip, smoke, and burn unevenly.

Your candles will burn longer if you refrigerate them for an hour or so before performing your rituals. Wrap them in foil or plastic first, to keep the wick from absorbing moisture.

Extinguish your candles with a snuffer. Alternatively, use a metal object, such as a spoon, to gently push the wick into the molten wax. This puts the candle out and eliminates smoke.

Once they have cooled, store your candles in zip-lock bags. This helps conserve any scent and protects them from dust. Candles are the most essential requirement in candle magic, and it is important that they are treated with respect and looked after properly.

Do not leave the room while your candles are burning. Be particularly careful when small children or pets are around. Remember that the containers your candles are in can become extremely hot. Treat everything with care.

Candle Holders

Choose candleholders that appeal to you. Everyone feels better when working with attractive implements. I like brass candle holders, because they are safe and tend to look slightly old-fashioned. I also use a metal tray on my altar, for safety. I avoid wooden and glass candlesticks. On two occasions, my glass candle holders unexpectedly broke in the middle of a ritual, and this could have caused a fire. As a result of these experiences, I am always cautious when dealing with fire.

Candle Snuffers

It is a tradition in candle magic that candles should not be blown out. This is because it is supposed to be an insult to the candle. I disagree with this, and sometimes deliberately blow out a candle, especially if I am sending the candle's energy to someone else. Most of the time, though, I use a brass candle snuffer. A candle snuffer adds to the ritual, as it symbolically seals in your intent. Candle snuffers are inexpensive, and can be found in larger candle stores. I found mine in an antique store, and I like the fact that people who were alive a hundred or more years ago used it to snuff out their candles. I sometimes wonder if other people used it for magical purposes.

Whenever possible I allow my candles to burn down completely. This is particularly desirable when a candle has been dedicated for a specific purpose. However, with the fast pace of life today, it is not always practical to leave a candle burning for several hours. Consequently, a candle snuffer is an essential item.

Pendulum

The pendulum is a useful tool that can be used for a large range of purposes. It is extremely helpful in candle magic. It can, for instance, tell you whether or not to perform a certain ritual at a specific time. It can provide additional feedback by answering questions you may have, such as which candles to use. A couple of days ago, I asked my pendulum if I should inscribe a certain candle I was planning to use. The pendulum gave a positive response, but then went on to tell me that I should inscribe a different message on the candle to the one I had intended.

A pendulum is a small weight attached to a piece of thread, string, or chain. A key or ring attached to a few inches of thread will work well as an impromptu pendulum. After working with a pendulum for a while, you will probably decide to get a specially made one, and these are readily available at new age and crystal stores.

Hold the pendulum by the thread, between your first finger and thumb, and allow the weight to hang freely. Most people find about three inches of thread is sufficient. Experiment with both hands. If you are right-handed, you will probably experience better results with your right hand. However, some people prefer to use the opposite hand to the one they write with. I find it helpful to rest my elbow on a table when asking questions to eliminate any accidental movements I may make with my arm.

Stop the movement of the weight with your free hand. Then ask the pendulum to give you a "yes" response.

It might take a little while for the pendulum to move, but within a minute or so it will move backward and forward, or from side to side, or perhaps make a circular movement, in either a clockwise or counterclockwise direction.

Once you have determined the positive response, stop the pendulum's movement and ask it to indicate "no." You can follow this by asking it to give you the "I don't know" and "I don't want to answer" movements.

Now you can ask it any question you wish that can be answered with one of these four responses. Practice as much as you can. This will prove the accuracy of the pendulum to you. Do not ask it frivolous questions. If you do, you are likely to receive equally frivolous responses. The pendulum is a wonderful magical tool, and should be treated with respect. My book, *Pendulum Magic for Beginners* (Llewellyn, 2002), deals with the subject in depth.

The pendulum can be used at every stage of candle magic. It can help you choose the right candles, for instance. You can test the degree of energy inside the candles after you have dressed and charged them. This is particularly important if you are using candles that were charged some time earlier. You can use your pendulum to check the right times at which to perform your rituals. You can assess the amount of power and energy in your rituals, and you can confirm that you have performed the ritual correctly.

Smudging

Smudging is a shamanic method of cleansing, purifying, and blessing an environment, such as the area around your personal altar. However, you can smudge your entire home, if you wish. You can also smudge people, animals, and anything else you wish.

The word *smudge* is an old English word that described the smoky fire that cattle were driven through to cleanse them of insects.

A smudge stick contains herbs, spices, or incense, tied up in a small bundle, which is lit. The smoke produced is brushed over and around any areas that need purification.

Rosemary, sage, sweetgrass, lavender, mugwort, and wormwood are all popular herbs for smudging. Tie your herbs in a small bundle with cotton thread, so that it resembles a large, fat cigar. Light one end and allow the sweet-smelling smoke to rise. Move the smudge stick around to allow the smoke to spread. Alternatively, fan it with a feather or fan. You should not blow as this is believed to create an opportunity for negative energies to enter the smoke.

You can also burn the herbs loosely, if you prefer. This creates an extremely hot mixture. Special care is needed when using a smudge stick or bundle, and a fireproof container is essential. A ceramic bowl containing sand is a useful item to deposit the smudge stick in after you have finished smudging. Remember that herbs continue to smolder for a long time after the fire has been put out.

Smudging your altar before use is an excellent way to focus your mind on the task you are about to do. Many magicians sprinkle water on the altar as well, believing that it concentrates their minds and also activates the altar.

Circle

The circle marks the perimeter of your sacred space where you will perform your candle magic. You can indicate the circle in many ways. You may use masking tape on the floor to mark out a circle with a diameter of about seven feet. You might mark a white circle on a sheet of material, making an effective portable circle. Alternatively, you might do as I do, and use a circular rug. Your altar, which is your magical workbench, is placed inside the circle.

Altar

An altar is a sacred place where you can perform your candle magic. Most people use a table or sideboard as an impromptu altar, and there is nothing wrong with this. For years I used a card table that was stored in a closet when I wasn't using it. However, there are benefits from having a special, designated place that is used solely for your magic. This is a personal sacred space for prayer, meditation, ritual, and magic. Intention is the key to all magic, and this also applies to the altar itself. If you set aside a space for magic, with the intention of using it only for this purpose, it will develop a character and spirituality of its own. Whenever you find yourself in this space, even if it is a corner of a large room, you will immediately feel centered and strong.

Your altar can be as elaborate or as simple as you wish. A coffee table works well. Many people prefer working standing up, and a sideboard might be a better choice for them. Make sure that the altar is aesthetically pleasing to you. The only essential requirement is a flat surface to work on, which means that you can use almost anything that appeals to you.

It is a good idea to consecrate your altar by smudging it, or bathing it in both sunlight and moonlight. To do this, put your altar outside on a sunny day for a few hours, and then allow the light from a full moon to bathe it for a few hours, too.

Some people cover their altar with a white silk cloth, which is often embroidered or decorated in some way. It is important that this cloth is used only for its designated purpose. I have met people who have cloths of various colors. They use the correct planetary color for the particular ritual they are performing. It would be insulting to also use these planetary cloths as tablecloths.

Many magicians have side tables beside their altars to hold any equipment that is needed for a particular ritual. You should use a side table only if it can fit comfortably inside your circle.

Some people like to keep specific items on their altars. Athamés, chalices, censers, pentacles, crystals, and wands are good examples. A Book of Shadows, tarot cards, and various other divination tools are also frequently found on altars. The items you keep on your altar are up to you. I use an altar cloth, and place on it only the items that are necessary for the ritual I am about to perform. Everything else is kept out of sight. This probably dates back to the days when I had to keep my interests secret.

I was taught that the altar should be positioned so that you face east when performing magic. (Black magicians face west, but we are concerned only with white magic in this book.) However, some people prefer to face north. Experiment, and see which direction is better for you.

I have my altar at the edge of the circle, but other magicians I know prefer to have it in the center. Again, this is a personal choice, and you should experiment to see which you prefer.

Safety Concerns

Anything to do with fire has the potential to be dangerous. It is important to have something under your candle holders for protection. A metal tray may not look glamorous on an altar, but it is an essential piece of equipment. A small fire extinguisher is also a good idea.

Now that you are familiar with the basic tools of candle magic, we can move on to color. Color has an important role to play in candle magic, as you'll see in the next chapter.

Three
Color

Color is a form of vibrational energy. Subconsciously, we all know how we react to different colors. Red, for instance, stimulates and excites us, while green is calming and soothing. Not long ago I read that violent prisoners become calm and easy to manage when housed in cells with pink walls. Color psychologists make good use of the effects that different colors have on us. Owners of fast food restaurants, for instance, know that certain colors make us eat quickly and then leave. The right color scheme in a factory increases productivity. Too much yellow in a room gives people headaches. Wearing different colors affects our confidence and behavior.

Many years ago, a friend of mine was asked to give a talk to the top managers of the corporation she worked for. She was terrified at the prospect, and I suggested that she wear some red to give her confidence. She bought a red suit, and gave a brilliant speech that is still being talked about many years later. She credits her success to the energy, confidence, and enthusiasm that the red gave her.

Colors can be used in all sorts of ways to stimulate, soothe, or confuse us, and this has a profound effect on us physically, mentally, and emotionally. Most of the time this is done subconsciously. Once you become aware of the colors around you, you will look at the world in a different way, and notice the subtle way in which colors are being used to influence you.

There are three primary colors: red, yellow, and blue. All the other colors are derived from these. Red symbolizes creative and generative power, vitality, and strength. It represents creativity and energy. Yellow symbolizes the astral and mental planes. It represents mind, light, and love. Blue symbolizes the higher mental and spiritual planes. It represents truth and spirituality. In Theosophical terms, red represents the will, yellow represents mind or spirit, and blue represents love.

The rainbow consists of seven colors:

Red

Planet: Sun

Golden Dawn attribution: Mars

Archangel: Gabriel

Element: Earth

Keyword: Energy

Red is a physical and emotional color. It is stimulating and exciting. It gives enthusiasm, ambition, confidence, determination, courage, energy, and desire. As it is the color of blood, it is sometimes called the spirit of life. It is useful in sports as it reduces fatigue and provides increased energy. Red is ambitious and enjoys a challenge. It is the color of the senses. It is powerful, which is why we "roll out the red carpet" when dignitaries visit. It can also indicate danger, the reason it is used on traffic lights and warning signs. This probably also explains the expression "seeing red."

Not surprisingly, red has also been related to passion and lust, as readers of Nathaniel Hawthorne's *The Scarlet Letter* will know. We talk about a "burning passion," as red is the color of fire. This belief can even be found in the Bible. "Though your sins be as scarlet, they shall be white as snow; though they be red like crimson, they shall be as wool" (Isaiah 1:18). A popular gift at Chinese weddings used to be a pair of large red candles to be burned in the bedroom. These are given to enhance passion in the marriage and also ensure a large number of children.[1]

You should use red candles if your desires are related to sex, love, physical energy, or health. Red candles should also be used for all ambitious requests.

Orange

Planet: Mercury

Golden Dawn attribution: Sun

Archangel: Zadkiel

Element: Water

Keyword: Tact, diplomacy

Orange combines the physicality of red with the intellect of yellow. Consequently, it is a sociable, friendly, warming color that enhances social occasions and aids good communication. Orange enjoys new ideas, and is full of the joys of life. It is energetic and enjoys physical activities. Orange relates to all close relationships, and is concerned with the happiness and well being of others. Orange is thoughtful, considerate, and kind. It also provides motivation and a sense of direction.

Orange candles are a good choice if you are experiencing difficulties with someone and your magic relates to this. Orange candles release blocked energies, repressed ideas, and stubbornness. An orange candle increases your ability to handle all the difficulties that occur in everyday life. Orange candles can also draw to you whatever it is that you desire.

Yellow

Planet: Mars

Golden Dawn attribution: Mercury

Archangel: Ariel and Oriel

Element: Fire

Keyword: Adaptability

Yellow provides us with warmth, joy, and optimism. Imagine how you feel when you see the sunshine again after a long winter. It is related to the intellect, and stimulates mental energy, granting wisdom and knowledge when applied correctly. Yellow is also full of the joys of life and relates to social activities, fun, pleasure, entertainment, and happiness. Yellow relates to communication, and helps stimulate conversation and good times.

There is a negative aspect of yellow. When someone is described as being "yellow," or having a "yellow streak," it indicates that he is a coward. Judas was sometimes painted with yellowish hair, as a sign of jealousy.

You should use a yellow candle if your magic concerns creativity, friendships, and fun. A yellow candle stimulates the mind, and helps concentration, memory, and self-expression.

Green

Planet: Mercury

Golden Dawn attribution: Venus

Archangel: Chamuel

Element: Earth

Keyword: Humanitarianism

Green provides harmony, stability, and emotional balance. It promotes new growth, and supports and cherishes others. It is emotionally soothing, tranquil, and peaceful. Green is friendly, cooperative, and peace-loving. It is refreshing, supportive, and healing. There is reference to this in the 23rd Psalm, when David wrote: "He maketh me to lie down in green pastures: he leadeth me beside the still waters."

Green is also practical, hard working, and goal oriented, which is why green candles symbolize money. People with a great deal of green in their auras gain great pleasure from having beautiful possessions and money in the bank. There is more green than any other color in nature. Green symbolizes fertility, new life, and growth. A "greenhorn" is someone who is young and inexperienced.

You should use green candles if your magic is concerned with money, prosperity, abundance, success, and good fortune. It is a good color to burn when looking for work, or seeking a pay rise.

Blue

Planet: Jupiter

Golden Dawn attribution: Moon

Archangel: Michael

Element: Water

Keyword: Truth

Blue is expansive. Think of blue sea and blue sky. This is why blue is related to versatility, travel, and distant places. Blue is never happy with the present, and is always seeking new worlds to conquer. Blue is also creative, calming, honest, sincere, and contemplative. It is related to self-employment, good ideas, and the future. The early Christians used blue to symbolize modesty, chastity, purity, and faith. This is why the Spanish chose the term "blueblood" to indicate their supposed superiority over the defeated Moors. When Moses and seventy of his elders saw the God of Israel, under his feet was "a paved work of a sapphire stone" (Exodus 25:11). The throne of God was also made of sapphire (Ezekial 1:26). The tablets that Moses was given on Mount Sinai are believed to be of blue stone. Even today, there are places where the color blue is used to avert the evil eye. Blue is still considered a highly spiritual color.

Blue is also highly protective. You should burn blue candles if you are experiencing negativity. You should also use them if your desires relate to travel, advancement, creative activities, or you need time for contemplation. Burning a blue candle in your bedroom for several minutes before going to bed will help you enjoy a good night's sleep. Put the candle out before getting into bed.

If you have seen Shakespeare's *Richard III*, you may remember the scene where the Ghost of Buckingham comes into a room lit with blue candlelight. There was an old English belief that a candle burning with a blue flame brought bad luck, and Shakespeare used this piece of folklore to add power to the scene. It does not relate to candle magic.

Blue can also be cold. The blue ocean is cold and deep. When we feel "blue" or experience a "blue Monday" we are extending the coldness to also mean depression or illness.

Indigo

Planet: Neptune

Golden Dawn attribution: Saturn

Archangel: Raphael

Keyword: Integrity, Wisdom

Indigo is calming, purifying, spiritual, and highly intuitive. It is caring, nurturing, concerned, supportive, and thoughtful. It is practical, down-to-earth, and capable, and uses these skills to help others. Service to humanity is an important aspect of the color indigo.

True indigo candles are hard to find, but dark blue candles make an effective substitute. They should be burned if your magic involves helping others, especially family members. They can also be used to help you develop your psychic potential.

Violet

Planet: Saturn

Golden Dawn attribution: Jupiter

Archangel: Jophiel

Keyword: Inspiration, Intuition

Violet is related to the higher self, intuition, and unlimited potentials. It is concerned with philosophy, spiritual growth, religion, and the occult. It is inspirational, and stimulates the intuition. It is the color of the mystic. People with a large amount of violet in their auras are sensitive and extremely aware. They need a great deal of time on their own. Violet is an extremely restful color. Leonardo da Vinci wrote: "Meditation is ten times greater under a violet light, especially if falling through the stained glass window of a church."[2] It is believed that Wagner worked in a room containing a large amount of violet, including violet-colored drapes, when he composed his uplifting, spiritually inspired music.[3]

Violet or purple candles should be used if your magic is concerned with knowledge, spirituality, magic, or psychic development.

In addition to the rainbow colors, there are other colors that you are likely to need in your candle magic:

Pink

Pink contains many of the qualities of red, but in a softer, gentler form. It relates to love, affection, and warmth. It is nurturing, soothing, compassionate, and revitalizing.

Pink candles should be used if your magic is concerned with love, loyalty, integrity, and good intentions. An interesting use for pink candles is to burn them to encourage self-healing and self-love. We all need to nurture ourselves at times, and a ritual involving pink candles is not an indulgence, but a necessity to help restore mind, body, and soul.

Magenta

Magenta is the combination of crimson and violet. Consequently, it possesses some of the qualities of red and violet. It is an important color for letting go of the past. It relates to love, beauty, and self-respect—and it also strengthens the aura. Magenta candles should be used if your desires are related to leaving the past behind, self-esteem issues, and confidence.

Brown

Brown is related to the earth. Consequently, it is associated with security, property, and real estate. It is also connected with sorrow. Brown is reliable, conservative, unchanging, stubborn, and obliging. Brown candles should be used if your magic is connected with real estate, or concerns making amends for a wrong you have done. Brown can eliminate fears, stresses, anxieties, and uncertainties, as it strengthens and stabilizes the emotions. Brown is also related to animals. Consequently, a brown candle is a good choice when you are doing any form of healing magic for a pet, or any other animal.

White

The Tibetans believed that gods were white, and devils were black.[4] White is the color of unrefracted light, and is considered as important as gold. Aaron, the high priest, wore white robes. Later, white came to symbolize the Resurrection, which is why, in some parts of the world, it is used at funerals. White is pure, vibrant, and energetic. It relates to purity, innocence, and truth. In the East, the lotus flower is considered the symbol of innocence, perfection, and purity. It is one of the eight emblems of Buddhism. Not coincidentally, it happens to be white. The color white eliminates negative feelings and encourages a positive approach to life. Although white candles are usually burned for purification and protection purposes, white is an excellent color for any purpose. Whenever you are in doubt about which color candle to choose, or find it impossible to obtain the color you desire, use white.

Black

Many people consider black to be a negative or sinister color. However, it can also be sophisticated, worldly, and surprising. It is related to secrets and protection. You should not use black candles if you consider them evil or dangerous. Black candles contain enormous power, and can be used in magic where you are attempting to discover a secret, or are trying to determine the truth about something. Black candles can also be used whenever you want to draw out negative energies, such as an illness. Black candles should not be used by children, or by people who are emotionally drained. This is because black contains powerful energies that need to be handled carefully.

Silver

Silver is concerned with inner growth, intuition, beauty, and the arts. You should burn silver candles if your magic relates to any of these.

Gold

Gold is majestic, regal, and powerful. Kings wear gold crowns, and golden halos surround the heads of saints. Gold was sacred to the Mayans, Incas, and Aztecs because they worshipped the sun. Gold relates to wealth, prosperity, and abundance. You should choose a gold candle if your magic relates to large scale undertakings, new directions, and challenging opportunities.

Color Correspondences

The Hermetic Order of the Golden Dawn was established in London in 1888 by Dr. Wynn Westcott, S. L. MacGregor Mathers, Dr. W. R. Woodman, and the Rev. A. F. A. Woodford. Its members included William Butler Yeats, George Bernard Shaw, Aleister Crowley, and Arthur Edward Waite. The Order aimed to teach "the principles of occult Science and the Magic of Hermes." As well as coming up with their own list of colors for the planets, they also assigned certain colors to the signs of the zodiac.

Aries: Scarlet

Taurus: Red-orange

Gemini: Orange

Cancer: Amber

Leo: Yellow, greenish
Virgo: Green, yellowish
Libra: Emerald green
Scorpio: Green-blue
Sagittarius: Blue
Capricorn: Indigo
Aquarius: Violet
Pisces: Crimson

Here is a more traditional list of zodiac colors:
Aries: Yellow
Taurus: Indigo
Gemini: Green
Cancer: Orange
Leo: Red
Virgo: Green
Libra: Indigo
Scorpio: Yellow
Sagittarius: Blue
Capricorn: Violet
Aquarius: Violet
Pisces: Blue

Here is yet another popular list of associations:

Aries: Red

Taurus: Green

Gemini: Yellow

Cancer: Silver

Leo: Gold

Virgo: Brown

Libra: Blue

Scorpio: Deep red

Sagittarius: Purple

Capricorn: Black

Aquarius: Blue

Pisces: Violet

Experiment with different colored candles to find out which group of associations you prefer. You can use zodiacal candles to represent yourself and other people when performing candle magic.

Now that you know something of the meaning of the colors, you can start using this knowledge to help your life in many ways. In the next chapter we will discuss how burning a single candle, of the right color, can enhance every aspect of your life.

Four

Magic with a Single Candle

Numerous experiments have demonstrated how people are affected emotionally by different colors.[1] This has nothing to do with personal color preferences, but relates purely to the effects different colors have on people. Almost everyone, for instance, finds red stimulating, and violet calming. Red has been shown to raise blood pressure, while green can soothe and calm the emotions. This information is used all the time in color healing, and also plays a major role in emotional healing using a single candle.

You have probably already experienced emotional healing with a candle or candles, without knowing it. Whenever you sit down to a candlelit dinner you experience some of the benefits of candle magic. This might be more profound than you think. At one of my workshops, a man told me a sad story. When he and his wife first got married, they ate dinner at a candlelit table every night. Gradually, they stopped using the candle, and a year or so later they separated. Afterward, the man realized that the passion left their marriage at about the same time that they stopped lighting the candle. Lighting a candle can really light his and her fire.

There is also something special about using a single candle. A lighted candle is a reminder that there is one universal spirit, or God, in the universe. Psalm 18:28 says: "For thou will light my candle: the Lord my God will enlighten my darkness." A similar idea can also be found in Job 29:3: "When his candle shined upon my head, and when by his light I walked through darkness." In Proverbs 20:27 we read: "The spirit of man is the candle of the Lord."

Emotional Healing Magic

All you need to perform emotional healing with a single candle is a variety of different colored candles. To achieve the best results, you should do these experiments on your own. Choose a time when you will not be interrupted. I prefer to do this at night, as the room needs to be dimly lit. If you are doing this during the day, pull down the blinds or draw the curtains. You might like to temporarily disconnect the telephone as well.

Clear a space to act as an altar, and place the particular candle you feel will help you in the center. Place a comfortable chair about six feet from the candle. When you sit on it, you should be able to look directly at the candle flame, without raising or lowering your head. When I was a teenager, many years ago, I regularly visited Goodey's Bookshop, at that time the only New Age bookstore in my city. Frank Goodey, the owner, was a gentle, caring man who gave wonderful advice. He suggested that when I sit down, the flame of the candle should be in line with my third eye. Another useful piece of advice he gave me was to place a mirror under certain candles, because the mirror doubles the power of the candle.

Light the candle and sit down on the chair. Gaze at the candle flame, and think about why you are performing the ritual. If you are burning a red candle because you are lacking in energy, think how wonderful life will be when you are fully restored. See yourself doing a variety of physically draining tasks, but with plenty of energy left over once you're finished. Look at the flame and imagine the red of the candle expanding until it encompasses the entire room. Visualize yourself totally surrounded in red, and feel the red energy gradually revitalizing every cell of your body.

Continue gazing at the flame until you feel yourself totally bathed in red. Hold this feeling for as long as you can. When it starts to fade, say "thank you" out loud. Stretch and take a few deep breaths before standing up. If possible, leave the candle to burn itself out. Otherwise, snuff out the candle before carrying on with your day.

Many people say that you should never blow out a candle when doing candle magic. This is because it is believed to be insulting to the fire elements. I must confess that sometimes I deliberately blow my candles out. When you blow out a candle you add the air element to the fire element. However, most of the time I use a candle snuffer or my fingers to put the candle out. Use whichever method feels right for you at the time. Sometimes it will seem right to snuff the candle, while at other times it will seem perfectly appropriate to blow it out.

You will feel the results of this experiment immediately. The whole process takes between ten and thirty minutes, depending on your powers of visualization.

You can do this one-candle exercise as often as you wish. Here are some of the feelings and attitudes that can be altered with this exercise.

Red

Use a red candle if you are lacking in energy, confidence, or passion. You can also use it if you are feeling rejected or unworthy. Red helps eliminate pessimism and negative attitudes.

Orange

Use an orange candle if you lack vitality or motivation. Orange can also be used if you have difficulty in goal-setting, or don't know which direction to move in. It can also be used to cure fear, doubt, and worry.

Yellow

Use a yellow candle if you are feeling lonely, helpless, or depressed. Yellow can also help enhance your communication skills, and encourage honest, open communication, especially in relationships. Yellow should also be used whenever you feel hemmed in, limited, or frustrated.

Green

Use a green candle when you feel confused, angry, or out of control. Green also helps relieve stress, tension, resentment, and impatience. Green is useful if you are co-dependent, or feel emotionally unstable.

Blue

Use a blue candle if you are feeling indecisive, nervous, or unable to think clearly. A blue candle will also help if you are lacking in faith, hope, or courage. Fear of flying, and other forms of travel, can be helped by burning a blue candle.

Indigo

Use an indigo candle if you are lacking faith or spiritual direction. Indigo can also aid concentration and memory. Indigo is a good choice if you are feeling overwhelmed with responsibilities. Family difficulties can also be eased by burning an indigo candle.

Violet

Use a violet candle when you feel the need for inner peace. Violet eases feelings of guilt, increases a sense of self-worth, and nurtures the soul.

Pink

Burn a pink candle if you find it hard to give or receive love. Pink also helps release emotional traumas, and feelings of worthlessness and inadequacy.

Gray

Use a gray candle when you are suffering from prolonged stress, or mental exhaustion. Gray can help when you feel like giving up, or walking away from a problem.

Silver

Use a silver candle if you feel that you are not doing as well as you should, or could, be. Silver can help you gain confidence and increased self-esteem.

Gold

Use a gold candle if you have a fear of success, or doubt your worthiness of success. Gold is also useful if you are having difficulty in finding the right areas for progress, or have negative feelings about money.

White

You can use a white candle at any time, for any problem. Whenever you are unsure about which color candle to use, choose a white one.

A white candle can also be used to eliminate worry, and when you feel the need for additional protection.

Mandala Candle Healing

The emotional healing exercise can be taken a step further by using a mandala to determine the underlying psychological causes behind the emotions.

A mandala is a design drawn around a central point. In fact, "mandala" is the Sanskrit word for circle and center. This shows that a mandala represents both the interior world of the mind and the body (center), and the outer world (circle). A mandala symbolizes the universe. When you create a mandala you are putting your own personal energies into it. This fulfills the famous axiom "as above, so below," as you are putting yourself, the microcosm, into the mandala, which symbolizes the universe (macrocosm). In effect, you are traveling from the mundane, everyday world to the serene, blissful inner self, enabling you to understand yourself and your relationship with the universe more clearly.

In Tibet, mandalas are both works of art and powerful meditation tools. Their famous sand paintings are called *dul-tson-kyil-khor*, which means "mandala of colored sand." Creating one of these brings peace and healing. Once it is complete, the sand is swept up and poured into a river, allowing the healing energies to spread out across the world.

Hindu mandalas, known as pictorial yantras, are sacred objects that are used for meditation purposes. By focusing on the *bindu* in the center, the meditator aims to center his or her self.

The beautiful rose windows found in many churches are essentially mandalas. The famous mystic Saint Hildegard of Bingen (1098–1179) expressed her visions in both pictures and music. In one of her visions she saw God on a throne in the center of a huge mandala. He had a large wheel at his heart, and this expanded out to create a mandala that completely encircled the entire universe.

The Native American medicine wheel is a mandala. It consists of a cross within a circle. This represents the four seasons, four directions, and the four elements. When you are born, you symbolically start in the east and make your way around the circle as many times as are necessary until you return to spirit.

The Native American dream catcher is also a mandala. This is a spiral web-shaped instrument that catches good dreams, and allows bad dreams to pass through the web, so they will not be remembered.

The Navajo people create healing mandalas of sand, corn, pollen, petals, and charcoal, known as *iikááh*. This means "where the spirits come and go." The mandala is constructed during the day, and at nightfall the patient sits down in the center. The healer sings a story about bringing back harmony, while the patient thinks about how he or she has left the path, and needs to walk in a different direction in future to maintain good health and happiness. Finally, the spirits in the mandala drain the sickness out of the patient and into the mandala. This is carefully disposed of, and the now healed patient is able to progress with his or her life.

These examples show how important the mandala has been, and still is, to the well being of the world.

It was Carl G. Jung (1875–1961) who reintroduced the mandala to the West. He began drawing a mandala every day, and discovered how accurately it expressed his thoughts and feelings. He studied it for more than a decade before making his discoveries public. Jung considered the mandala to be an archetypal symbol that signified "wholeness of self."[2] He believed that the circular form of the mandala showed that everyone has an instinctive drive toward a satisfying wholeness, or completion. When he started using them with his patients, he found that many of them, including children, spontaneously drew circular designs that gave them feelings of peace, in the midst of the crisis they were in. Creating a mandala is a highly satisfying and enriching experience, which is why they are used as meditation tools.

For this exercise you need about a dozen colored pencils, crayons, or markers, a large sheet of paper, and a candle of the correct color for the healing you are about to undertake. You might like to use a plate to draw an outline of a circle on the sheet of paper before you start. Most mandalas are circular, as the circle is the symbol of wholeness and unity. However, there is no need to adhere to this if you do not want to. The shape you decide on can be anything you wish, and you should follow your feelings and intuition to decide this. You might choose a square, triangle, octagon, or any other shape that appeals at the time.

Set up your altar as before. You need enough room in front of the candle for the sheet of paper on which you will be drawing your mandala. I like to draw mandalas while kneeling in front of the altar. However, that is a personal preference, and you might prefer to sit or stand while you work.

Light the candle, and go through the emotional healing experiment again. When you reach the stage where you imagine yourself totally surrounded and full of the color of the candle, pick up one of the writing implements and draw your mandala. Use whatever colors feel right to you. Do not think about the process as you construct your mandala. Create a design or drawing around the central spot. You might draw a series of shapes, and then color them in. You might draw one shape of a particular color before creating another shape of a different color. There are no rules, and no right or wrong way to do this. It is best to create your mandala with as little thought as possible. Enjoy the process.

Continue with your mandala until you feel that it is finished, or until you can no longer visualize the color of the candle inside you.

Finish the experiment by saying "thank you" to the universal forces, and then snuff the candle out.

You can look at your mandala right away, or put it aside to study later. When you look at the colors and symbols you used you will be amazed at what the mandala has to tell you about your inner life. Your mandala is a map of your inner reality, and clearly reveals your state of mind at the time you created it.

Creating a mandala gives you access to your personal center deep inside, and enables you to contact your higher self. When you create a mandala you are releasing your inner self into the design. Healing takes place when you take it back into yourself by studying it afterward. In fact, the more mandalas you create, the more self-healing you will do, as each time you make one you will release unwanted aspects of your being. Mandalas reveal the truth of where you are at the moment you construct them. Consequently, you can use them to let go of anything that is painful or hurtful, and to follow what is wholesome and good. By changing your thoughts as a result of this process, you can change your life.

Creating mandalas will also help you develop spiritually and intuitively. A friend of mine draws a mandala at the start of every month. She says that by creating them on a regular basis she has become much more aware of the gradual changes that take place in her life than she would have been otherwise. She considers them to be "gentle therapy."

You might like to keep your mandalas for future reference. Date them and keep them in a folder. If you were feeling depressed or negative at the time you created them, some of your mandalas might feel gloomy and bleak. Do not worry about this. The act of creating them was a healing exercise that removed negativity from your system.

You may not want to keep all, or any, of the negative mandalas. If this is the case, light a white candle and burn the mandala while thanking it for releasing the negativity. When you dispose of it in this way, you purify the mandala as you return it to the universe.

Single Candle Rituals

Make a Wish Ritual

Write down your desire or wish on a sheet of paper. It is important that the paper has not been used for any other purpose beforehand. Fold the paper into quarters and place it under a candlestick. Choose a candle of a color that relates to your request. Place it in the candleholder and light it.

Sit down in a comfortable chair and watch the candle burn. Visualize as clearly as you can whatever it is you have requested. Imagine it already in your possession. Watch the flickering flame. Observe the patterns it makes, and the changing colors that appear. If your eyes get tired, look at the candle and think about why you chose that particular color.

Concentrate on your wish for as long as you can. When you feel the time is right, take the sheet of paper with your wish written on it from under the candlestick and burn it in the flame. As the paper burns, visualize your request going out into the universe, where it will be answered.

Snuff out the candle. If it still contains enough wax to repeat the ritual later on, put it away carefully. Remember, though, that the candle can be used again only for sending out the same wish. If you want to request something else, you need to use a fresh candle.

A Notch a Day

This is a ritual that can last for as many days as you wish. It should be reserved for important requests, rather than trivial demands. Inscribe a series of notches on a candle to mark out periods of time. Usually, a notch a day is performed for three to seven days. Write down your desire and place it under the candle. Light your candle at the same time each day, and keep it burning until it has burned down one notch. Focus on your goal the whole time the candle is burning. You will discover that the daily repetition increases the potency of your request.

Circle Dance

A friend of mine loves this ritual, as she says it helps her lose weight while she is performing her magic. Start by thinking of your purpose in holding the ritual, and then write a simple rhyme to express what you desire. It makes no difference what this rhyme is like, as long as you find it easy to remember. I find humorous rhymes work extremely well. Here is an example of this sort of simple rhyme:

I need a raise in pay,
And I want it today.
I know I'm not a bard,
But without it life is hard,
So I need, I need, I need, I need, I need,
I need a raise in pay.

Place a small candle on a small table, and make sure that there is plenty of room around it. Wear loose-fitting clothes, or nothing at all, if you prefer. If you are doing this in the daytime, darken the room, so that the only light will come from the candle.

Light the candle, and start to dance around the table. After you have danced around the table three times, start repeating your rhyme as you dance. Pause whenever you need to stop for breath, but keep on repeating the rhyme. Keep on doing this until the candle burns out.

Take several deep breaths, bow in all four directions, give thanks, and leave the room. The room should not be used for any other purpose for at least three hours after the ritual is finished.

Magical dance is one of the oldest, and easiest, methods of gaining contact with the universal energies. This, coupled with the rhyme, and the burning of the candle, makes for an extremely powerful ritual.

Start with a small candle. You will be amazed how long it takes a candle to burn down to nothing when you are dancing around it. This ritual is exhilarating, but can be exhausting. Do not overtire yourself. There are no rules about the dance. It can be simple or elaborate, depending on your previous experience, level of fitness, and energy at your disposal. No one will see what you are doing, so make your movements as outrageous and dramatic as you wish.

Count Your Blessings Ritual

No matter how difficult life can be at times, there are always things to be thankful for. This month-long ritual can help you become more positive in outlook, more grateful for what you do have, and more accepting of the ups and downs of life in general.

You will need to find a blessing tree. This is a branch, approximately six feet long, that you will use to hang your blessings on every day for a month. I prefer to use a branch that has fallen from a tree, rather than cut a branch off for this purpose. It makes no difference what tree it has come from, although some people claim that a branch from a fig tree is the most effective.

The reason for this is that the fig tree is full of symbolism. Adam and Eve covered themselves with fig leaves in the Garden of Eden (Genesis 3:7). The Promised Land was believed to be a land of vines and fig trees. Gautama Buddha meditated for six years in the wilderness, and finally received enlightenment while sitting under a Bodhi Tree (*ficus religiosa*). He also received nourishment from the figs that the tree produced. Consequently, the fig tree is sometimes known as the "tree of meditation." Romulus and Remus were believed to have been suckled under the protective branches of a fig tree, and the fig tree became an emblem of prosperity.

You will also need a candle. I prefer a slender white candle for this ritual. However, any color that pleases you will work well.

I prefer to hang my blessing tree horizontally in the corner of a room, where I can see it easily, but where it won't be in the way. You can place your blessing tree vertically in a pot, if you wish. There are no right or wrong ways to display your blessing tree.

Once a day, write down on a piece of paper something that you are grateful for. This is your blessing for the day. It can be anything at all. You might give thanks for life, for good health, for family and friends, for a promotion at work, for a good turn that someone did for you.

Read what you have written out loud, and then attach it to the blessing tree. Light a single candle, and place this near the tree. Sit down and stare into the flame as you think about the blessing. Do this for as long as you can. When you notice your attention is wandering, put the candle out, and carry on with your day.

Repeat this every day for a month. At the end of this time, you will have thirty blessings attached to your blessing tree. Some people find it hard to come up with thirty things to be grateful for. This is good, as it forces them to think about their lives, and discover blessings that they were not consciously aware of before.

Once the month is over, take all the blessings off the tree. Light the candle again, and read the first blessing out loud. Once you have done this, burn the paper in the candle flame. Repeat this with all of the blessings. Take your blessing tree outside and burn it also. You have now sent your blessings out into the universe, where they will gather more blessings to enhance every aspect of your life.

Candles for Love and Friendship

The term "holding a candle" for someone means that you are keen on that person. Lighting a candle for someone is even more powerful. You can light a candle at any time to send love, friendship, and healing to another person. If you are concerned or worried about someone, light a candle to send love and healing to him or her. You can do the same thing if someone is celebrating or has achieved something. You can burn a candle of congratulation for that person's achievement.

Choose the color according to the knowledge you have of the person you are burning the candle for, and your feelings at the time you are burning it.

These small rituals are made more effective if you blow out the candle and then say: "I am sending this blessing to you" followed by the person's name. The energy from the candle will reach the person you have named and will inspire and uplift them.

As you can see, a single candle can transform your life. However, the candle you choose has to be prepared carefully before using it for any magical purpose. This is covered in the next chapter.

Five

How to Prepare Your Candles

It is important that your candles are properly prepared before using them in any magic ritual. There is no knowing what negative energies they have been exposed to before coming into your possession. Often candles are dusty, or have been handled by a number of potential purchasers before you bought them. Consequently, your candles need to be cleaned and purified before use.

The most important part of this process is to dress or anoint your candles with oil. There are many commercially made oils available that have been prepared for specific purposes. These can be obtained from specialty candle and occult stores, and over the Internet. You will be amazed at the number of oils that are available. There are attraction oils, gambling oils, good luck oils, happiness oils, healing oils, horoscope oils, love oils, meditation oils, planetary oils, protection oils, seduction oils, and many more. Some of the suppliers offer ranges of several hundred oils. If you buy a commercially made oil, ensure that it is colorless, so that you can use it on candles of any color. Colored oils can only be used on a candle which is the same color as the oil.

Sometimes I buy a particular oil, but most of the time I use baby oil that I buy at my local supermarket. This works well for most purposes, and means that I don't need to store a large variety of different oils.

Here are some suggested oils for different purposes:

- To attract good luck: Fast Luck oil, or Good Fortune oil

- To attract someone or something to you: Attraction oil, or Magnet oil

- To advance in your career, or to find new employment: Success oil

- To enhance the memory, or to pass an exam: Mercury oil

- To gain courage: Geranium oil

- To heal yourself, or others: Balm of Gilead

- To obtain peace of mind: Myrrh oil

- To obtain urgently needed money: Horn of Plenty oil

- To obtain money for any purpose: Money-drawing oil, or Mint oil
- To obtain spiritual assistance: Holy oil, or any oil named after a saint
- To attract a long-lasting love relationship: Venus oil, or Rose Petal oil
- To attract a short-term sexual relationship: Jupiter oil
- To protect yourself, or others: Saint Michael oil
- To protect yourself from psychic attack: Spiritual Protection oil, Ultimate Security oil, or Jasmine oil

These are just a few of the many hundreds of oils that are commercially available. You can also make your own oils, if you wish. I recommend this, as you can add a great deal of additional power and potency to your goal by remaining focused on it while making the oil. Use only the best quality materials for this. Virgin or extra-virgin olive oil makes a good base, and you can add to it whatever is necessary to make the type of oil you require.

It is a good idea to bless any commercially made oils you buy, to eliminate any negativity that they may be hanging on to. Do this by facing east and holding the container of oil as high as you can with both hands. Say out loud: "I bless this oil and consecrate it for the purpose of (whatever your goal happens to be). My purpose is good, and I ask for divine protection on me, this oil, and my goal. Thank you."

Cleansing the Candle

Start by looking at the candle carefully. You may need to trim off any wax drippings, and scrape off any imperfections or dirty marks. You might want to wipe the candle with a tissue soaked in rubbing alcohol to remove any negative energies that the candle might be carrying. If you do this, rub from the base of the candle, up to the top. This draws any negative energies out of the candle. Allow the candles to dry naturally after cleansing them. After this, you might like to buff them with a polishing cloth to give them an attractive sheen.

Once you are satisfied that the candle is free of negativity, dust, and imperfections, you can start on the next stage.

Consecrating the Candle

This stage is optional. However, I generally do it as anything that gives additional power to the ritual is worthwhile. You need a sharp knife to carve a design into the side of the candle near the base. The knife should be used only for this purpose.

The design you carve into the candle depends entirely on you, and your goal. If you come from a Christian background, you might like to carve a cross on the side of the candle. Carve a vertical line first, carving in a downward direction. Follow this with the horizontal line, carving from left to right.

You might prefer to carve a pentagram on the side of the candle. This is an ancient symbol of protection. It also symbolizes the universal spirit bringing the four elements into balance. The top point of the pentagram depicts the spirit, and the other four points represent the four elements: fire, earth, air, and water.

Alternatively, you might like to carve something that symbolizes your goal. A dollar sign could be used, for example, if your goal was to attract money. A heart could be used to attract love.

If the candle represents a person, you might carve something that symbolizes him or her. This could be the person's name, horoscope sign, date of birth, or anything else that helps to further associate the candle with this person.

If you are using the candle to attract someone to you, you might inscribe on it certain qualities that you wish this person to have.

It makes no difference what symbol or design you carve into the candle, as long as it has meaning to you, and is related to your goal. Naturally, you must remain focused on your goal while you are inscribing your design onto the candle.

Dressing the Candle

Dressing your candles can be a messy business. It pays to wear old clothes, and work on a surface that can be easily cleaned afterward. Most of the time, I dress my candles outdoors, but naturally this depends on the weather. When I need to do it indoors, I work on the kitchen table. I don't think it is a good idea to prepare your candles on the same surface that you will be using as an altar later on.

Start by rubbing oil onto both of your hands. Hold the candle near the center, and, starting from the center rub the oil toward the top of the candle. It is important to rub in an upward direction only.

While doing this, think of your purpose in dressing the candle. This is the most important aspect of dressing a candle. While dressing it, you are imprinting your thoughts into the candle, and consecrating it for a particular purpose. Some people repeat an affirmation, or express their thoughts out loud, to help them focus on their goal. It is important that a candle is consecrated for a single purpose. If you are preparing it for prosperity, for instance, you should not also use it to attract a romantic relationship. The one exception to this is when you consecrate a candle for personal power. This candle can then be used for any positive purpose.

Once the top of the candle has been dressed, oil the bottom half of the candle in the same way, rubbing from the center downward to the base.

Some people prefer to rub upward, from the center to the top, once, and then rub the bottom half once, alternating between the two halves. This means that neither half of the candle can claim superiority over the other half. As I was taught to rub the top half first, followed by the bottom half, I always dress my candles this way.

There is another tradition, also, that says that when you are performing candle magic to bring something good into your life, you rub the candle from the top down to the base. Conversely, if you want to eliminate something negative from your life, rub the candle from the base up to the top.

In the end, it amounts to personal preference. Try all of these methods, and then stick to the one you prefer.

Naturally, the most important aspect of dressing your candles is to concentrate on your ultimate purpose. In comparison to this, the exact manner in which you dress your candles is unimportant.

Over the years, I have met a number of people who dislike handling oil, either because the process is messy, or the smell makes them feel ill. The remedy for this is to dress the candle with water, instead of oil. There are three ways of doing this. The first is to obtain a spray bottle, so that you can cover the entire candle with a mist of water, while you say an affirmation, or think of your goal. Alternatively, you can dip your right hand into a bowl of water and sprinkle the candle while thinking of your goal. The third method is to rub the candle with water, in exactly the same way you would if using oil.

Winding the Candle

I enjoy this final stage of candle preparation. Some people feel that it is unnecessary, but I find it helpful.

Hold your cleansed and dressed candle and think about how you are going to use it. Think of your goal as you wind a length of thin ribbon around the candle, starting at the bottom and finishing at the top. This binds your intention to the candle. Some people like to do this as the final stage of candle preparation. Others prefer to do it immediately before using the candle. I have no personal preference in this, and sometimes wind my candles as the final stage of preparing them, but equally as often do it immediately before using them.

Now that your candles have been cleansed, dressed, and wound, you can start using them for magic. You are probably anxious to prepare your candles, but before you do, you should also know the best times to burn them. That is the subject of the next chapter.

Six

Timing

The best time to perform your magic is when the universal forces are working in your favor. The purpose of this chapter is to help you determine the best times to perform your magic. This allows you to plan ahead, and determine a day and time that is perfect for your magic. This also gives you time to prepare yourself mentally, physically, emotionally, and spiritually, so that you will be able to focus all of your energies on your specific goal.

However, your schedule may not always give you the luxury of choosing certain hours in which to perform your magic. If the need is urgent, you may not be able to wait for a propitious time. When this happens, do your magic anyway. You can still use your knowledge of the correct times. If, for example, you are trying to attract a lover during the waning Moon (which means decrease), use this apparently negative aspect in a positive way. Include in your magic something to eliminate any obstacles that might be standing in your way. This is using the negativity in a positive way to help you achieve your goal. For example, if you are trying to establish peace between you and a neighbor, you would not normally do this on a day of Mars, but if you had no alternative, you could use the Martian energies to provide you with protection.

Naturally, it is better to use the right times when possible. For the best results, timing is of vital importance. There are a number of ways of doing this.

Cycles of the Moon

The Moon plays a major part in every aspect of our lives. It is responsible for the rise and fall of the tides, and even affects the sap in plants and trees. The term "lunatic" is named after the Moon, as people noticed the strange effect it had on some animals and people. The Moon even affects our weather.[1]

The Moon waxes as it grows from the new Moon to full Moon. This is the time to perform any magic that is concerned with growth, expansion, or increase.

The waning Moon is the period from the full Moon to the new Moon. This is the perfect time for any magic that is concerned with eliminating destructive energies or anything else that you no longer want in your life.

Days of the Week

Each day of the week is related to a particular planet, which in turn relates to a variety of different energies. It follows that these days are good times to perform magic that relates to these energies.

- Monday is ruled by the Moon; the Moon is concerned with healing, emotions, protection, purity, memory, and women; the color for Monday is white

- Tuesday is ruled by Mars; Mars is concerned with courage, loyalty, wealth, power, and force; the color for Tuesday is red

- Wednesday is ruled by Mercury; Mercury is concerned with communication, business, travel, thought, humor, and all forms of self-expression; the color for Wednesday is purple

- Thursday is ruled by Jupiter; Jupiter is concerned with ambition, expansion, abundance, success, generosity, honor, and growth; the color for Thursday is blue

- Friday is ruled by Venus; Venus is concerned with love, romance, sex, home and family, pleasure, and fun; the color for Friday is green

- Saturday is ruled by Saturn; Saturn is concerned with delays, obstacles, real estate, patience, and hard work; the color for Saturday is black

- Sunday is ruled by the Sun; the Sun is concerned with leadership, protection, prosperity, creativity, and success; the color for Sunday is yellow

Hours of the Day

The planetary hours allow us to determine the best time of any day to perform magic. The planetary hours do not follow the same hours that we do. The daytime is divided into twelve equal periods, from sunrise to sunset. In summer, these periods of time are longer than they are in winter. The same thing applies with the nighttime hours. In winter, the nighttime hours are longer than they are in summer. Fortunately, most daily newspapers give the times of sunrise and sunset. Once you know these times, you can divide the day into twelve equal periods, known as planetary hours. You can also do this for the nighttime planetary hours. Remember that our calendar days begin at midnight and end at the following midnight. Planetary days start at sunrise and finish at sunrise the next day.

Each hour is connected to a particular planet, and takes on that planet's qualities. The planets for each hour can be found in Appendix C (p. 227). You will notice that the first hour of every day has the same planet as the day with which it is connected. The first planetary hour for Sunday, for example, is ruled by the Sun. The first hour for Monday is ruled by the Moon, and so on.

Now that you know about the Moon, planetary days, and planetary hours, you can combine this knowledge to determine the best time for you to perform your magic. Let's assume, for example, you are wanting more money.

Naturally, the best time to do a spell of this sort would be when the Moon is waxing, as you want increase. You would probably also choose to perform your magic on a Thursday, and would choose one of the hours of Jupiter (1, 8, 15, or 22).

It is interesting to note that the planetary days and hours have been used by magicians for more than two thousand years. Astrological records going back to 27 BCE show that, even then, people were using the same order of planets, and the same methods of timing, that we use today.[2]

The Solar Year

In practice, this is sufficient for virtually every situation. However, if you are planning well ahead, you might also choose to use the solar year in the same way as the waxing and waning Moon. For spells involving expansion and increase, use the period from Yule to Midsummer. For decrease, do your magic between Midsummer and Yule.

Cosmic Vibration

What we have covered so far are the traditional methods of timing. Now we come to a method that was taught to me more than thirty-five years ago. It is not original to me, but I have never seen it in print anywhere.

I am a great believer in serendipity. This is when advantageous things occur, apparently by accident. I believe that serendipitous happenings are not accidental at all, but occur because we have subconsciously sent out into the universe the correct energies that allow it to happen. I was traveling from London to Glasgow, and had bought a book called *Color Psychology and Color Therapy* by Faber Birren to read on the train. I was so engrossed in the book that I didn't look up when someone came into the compartment and sat down opposite me. After a few minutes, I heard a man reciting the colors of the rainbow out loud. Naturally, I looked up and the man sitting opposite beamed at me. He had a weather-beaten face, long, stringy-looking gray hair, and penetrating eyes. He was probably in his middle fifties, but I was twenty at the time and thought he looked old.

"That's a good book," he said, pointing a stubby finger at the book I'd been reading. "Sound man, Faber Birren."

"Yes," I agreed. "I don't know anything about him."

"Interested in color, though?"

"I guess so. It just looked like an interesting book."

"You'd have bought it at Watkins'."

Watkins Bookshop is a famous occult bookstore in London. Even today, it is still the first place I visit whenever I go to London.

Once he had established that I was interested in psychic matters, the man leaned forward and talked almost all the way to Scotland. His name was Herbert Fernyhough. He told me that he had been born to wealthy parents, and had never had to work. He lived on a small country estate, where he spent most of his time reading and studying. One of the many things he talked about on the long train ride was cosmic energy and how humanity would take a giant leap forward if everybody was taught how to use their cosmic vibration properly. I had to admit that I had no idea what cosmic vibration was.

"It's energy," he told me, waving his arms around to emphasize his words. "Your vibration was determined by your day of birth."

He told me that there are three groups of vibrations. These are:

Group One: People born on the 1st, 5th, 7th, 10th, 14th, 16th, 19th, 23rd, 25th, or 28th of any month

Group Two: People born on the 2nd, 4th, 8th, 11th, 13th, 17th, 20th, 22nd, 26th, 29th, or 31st of any month

Group Three: People born on the 3rd, 6th, 9th, 12th, 15th, 18th, 21st, 24th, 27th, or 30th of any month

Any dates in the group that you belong to are good for you. If you were born on July 4, for example, you would belong to group two. This means that the best days for you to perform candle magic are all the days listed in group two. October 2 and 4 would be good, but the 3rd would not be, as three is not in group two.

These lists of dates may look intimidating at first, but they are easy to remember. The dates in group one are 1, 5, and 7, plus any other numbers that reduce down to these numbers when added together. Consequently, 25 is in this group, because 2 + 5 = 7. The dates in group two are 2, 4, and 8, plus any other numbers that reduce down to these numbers when added together. This is why 29 is in this group. 2 + 9 = 11, and 1 + 1 = 2. The same thing applies with group three. In this group are number 3, 6, and 9, plus any other numbers that reduce down to these. 24 is in this group as 2 + 4 = 6.

We can also further divide these groups into mental, physical, and spiritual days. You should perform magic that relates to knowledge, learning, and communication on the mental days. The physical days refer to more than physical energy. They are the best days to work on increase. This could be more money, more energy, more friends, more anything. The spiritual days are the best days for magic that is concerned with healing yourself, and others. They are also the best days for meditation, spiritual development, and intuition.

Group One

Born on the 1st of any month
Mental days: 10th, 14th, 16th, and 19th
Physical days: 23rd, 25th, and 28th
Spiritual days: 1st, 5th, and 7th

Born on the 5th of any month
Mental days: 16th, 19th, 23rd, and 25th
Physical days: 1st, 5th, and 28th
Spiritual days: 7th, 10th, and 14th

Born on the 7th of any month
Mental days: 23rd, 25th, and 28th
Physical days: 1st, 5th, and 7th
Spiritual days: 10th, 14th, 16th, and 19th

Born on the 10th of any month
Mental days: 1st, 5th, and 28th
Physical days: 7th, 10th, and 14th
Spiritual days: 16th, 19th, 23rd, and 25th

Born on the 14th of any month
Mental days: 1st, 5th, and 7th
Physical days: 10th, 14th, 16th, and 19th
Spiritual days: 23rd, 25th, and 28th

Born on the 16th of any month
Mental days: 14th, 16th, 19th, and 23rd
Physical days: 1st, 25th, and 28th
Spiritual days: 5th, 7th, and 10th

Born on the 19th of any month
Mental days: 19th, 23rd, 25th, and 28th
Physical days: 1st and 5th
Spiritual days: 7th, 10th, 14th, and 16th

Born on the 23rd of any month
Mental days: 1st, 25th, and 28th
Physical days: 5th, 7th, and 10th
Spiritual days: 14th, 16th, 19th, and 23rd

Born on the 25th of any month
Mental days: 1st and 5th
Physical days: 7th, 10th, 14th, and 16th
Spiritual days: 19th, 23rd, 25th, and 28th

Born on the 28th of any month
Mental days: 5th, 7th, and 10th
Physical days: 14th, 16th, 19th, and 23rd
Spiritual days: 1st, 25th, and 28th

Group Two

Born on the 2nd of any month
Mental days: 13th, 17th, 20th, and 22nd
Physical days: 26th, 29th, and 31st
Spiritual days: 2nd, 4th, 8th, and 11th

Born on the 4th of any month
Mental days: 20th, 22nd, 26th, and 29th
Physical days: 2nd, 4th, and 31st
Spiritual days: 8th, 11th, 13th, and 17th

Born on the 8th of any month
Mental days: 26th, 29th, and 31st
Physical days: 2nd, 4th, 8th, and 11th
Spiritual days: 13th, 17th, 20th, and 22nd

Born on the 11th of any month
Mental days: 2nd, 4th, and 31st
Physical days: 8th, 11th, 13th, and 17th
Spiritual days: 20th, 22nd, 26th, and 29th

Born on the 13th of any month
Mental days: 2nd, 4th, 8th, and 11th
Physical days: 13th, 17th, 20th, and 22nd
Spiritual days: 26th, 29th, and 31st

Born on the 17th of any month
Mental days: 17th, 20th, 22nd, and 26th

Physical days: 2nd, 29th, and 31st
Spiritual days: 4th, 8th, 11th, and 13th

Born on the 20th of any month
Mental days: 22nd, 26th, 29th, and 31st
Physical days: 2nd, 4th, and 8th
Spiritual days: 11th, 13th, 17th, and 20th

Born on the 22nd of any month
Mental days: 2nd, 29th, and 31st
Physical days: 4th, 8th, 11th, and 13th
Spiritual days: 17th, 20th, 22nd, and 26th

Born on the 26th of any month
Mental days: 2nd, 4th, and 8th
Physical days: 11th, 13th, 17th, and 20th
Spiritual days: 22nd, 26th, 29th, and 31st

Born on the 29th of any month
Mental days: 4th, 8th, 11th, and 13th
Physical days: 17th, 20th, 22nd, and 26th
Spiritual days: 2nd, 29th, and 31st

Born on the 31st of any month
Mental days: 8th, 11th, 13th, and 17th
Physical days: 20th, 22nd, 26th, and 31st
Spiritual days: 2nd, 4th, and 31st

Group Three

Born on the 3rd of any month
Mental days: 15th, 18th, 21st, and 24th
Physical days: 27th, and 30th
Spiritual days: 3rd, 6th, 9th, and 12th

Born on the 6th of any month
Mental days: 21st, 24th, 27th, and 30th
Physical days: 3rd and 6th
Spiritual days: 9th, 12th, 15th, and 18th

Born on the 9th of any month
Mental days: 27th and 30th
Physical days: 3rd, 6th, 9th, and 12th
Spiritual days: 15th, 18th, 21st, and 24th

Born on the 12th of any month
Mental days: 3rd and 6th
Physical days: 9th, 12th, 15th, and 18th
Spiritual days: 21st, 24th, 27th, and 30th

Born on the 15th of any month
Mental days: 3rd, 6th, 9th, and 12th
Physical days: 15th, 18th, 21st, and 24th
Spiritual days: 27th and 30th

Born on the 18th of any month
Mental days: 18th, 21st, 24th, and 27th
Physical days: 3rd and 30th
Spiritual days: 6th, 9th, 12th, and 15th

Born on the 21st of any month
Mental days: 24th, 27th, and 30th
Physical days: 3rd, 6th, and 9th
Spiritual days: 12th, 15th, 18th, and 21st

Born on the 24th of any month
Mental days: 3rd and 30th
Physical days: 6th, 9th, 12th, and 15th
Spiritual days: 18th, 21st, 24th, and 27th

Born on the 27th of any month
Mental days: 3rd, 6th, and 9th
Physical days: 12th, 15th, 18th, and 21st
Spiritual days: 24th, 27th, and 30th

Born on the 30th of any month
Mental days: 6th, 9th, 12th, and 15th
Physical days: 18th, 21st, 24th, and 27th
Spiritual days: 3rd and 30th

If you have studied numerology, you will know that the three groups are known as the three concords. The 1, 5, 7 group is known as the scientific concord, the 2, 4, 8, 11 group is called the business concord, and the 3, 6, 9 group is called the artistic concord. Although I already knew that when I met Mr. Fernyhough, I had never seen them used in this way to determine the best times for magic. If I had not happened to meet Mr. Fernyhough on the train, I would probably still not know of this system.

I immediately began experimenting with it, and found that it gave excellent results. Consequently, it is the system I use most of the time.

Fatality of Days

This is another method of determining fortunate and unfortunate days, and is based on the day of the month in which the full moon occurs. Arthur Edward Waite wrote that this system is "very ancient, and has been tested to such an extent that it is considered accurate by most astrologers."[3] The word *fatality* in "fatality of days" does not mean death. This alternative interpretation of the word means fate or destiny.

To determine the fortunate days, you count the numbers of days to the end of the month from the full moon. You then multiply this number by the day the full moon occurred. For example, assume that full moon occurred on September 18. As September has thirty days, there are twelve days after the 18th. Multiply the 18 by these 12 days, which gives you a total of 216. This is now turned into two fortunate days: the 2nd and 16th. If the total happened to be 261, the lucky days would still be the same, as the last two numbers would have to be transposed to create a date. If the total happened to be 266, the lucky days would be the 2nd and 6th, and the 6th would be especially fortunate, as it appeared twice.

We also need to work out the unfortunate days, as it is possible for a particular day to be both fortunate and unfortunate. When this occurs, that particular date is ignored.

The unfortunate days are determined by counting backward from the full moon to the first of the month. To continue with our example of the full moon being on the 18th, we count back seventeen days. Consequently, the unfortunate days are determined by multiplying 17 x 18 = 306. The unfortunate days for this particular September are 3 and 6. As neither of these are the same as the fortunate days, we can safely take note of all four dates.

The fortunate days are excellent for any form of magic that involves increase. You should not perform magic on the unfortunate days, except in an emergency, or if your magic involves eliminating something from your life.

Numerology

Another method for choosing the right days for magic is to use numerology to determine your personal days. The first stage is to determine your personal year. This is done by adding up your day and month of birth, and adding this to the current year. If you were born on September 17, for instance, and the current year is 2004, you would create the following sum:

Month of birth	9
Day of birth	17
Current year	2004
	2030

This is reduced down to a single digit: $2 + 0 + 3 + 0 = 5$. In this example, 5 would be your personal year.

If you add the current month to the personal year, and again bring it down to a single digit, you will find your personal month. Let's assume it is July. We add 7 (for July) to the 5 personal year. This gives us 12, which reduces down to 3 $(1 + 2 = 3)$. You are in a 3 personal month.

Finally, you add the current day to the personal month, and again reduce it down to a single digit. Let's assume it is the 19th of the month. We add 19 to the 3 personal month, which gives us 22. $2 + 2 = 4$. You are in a 4 personal day.

Here's another example. Let's suppose that your birthday is on March 23, and you want to find your personal day number for August 29, 2006. You first find your personal year, followed by the personal month, and finally personal day.

Month of birth	3
Day of birth	23
Current year	2006
	2032

Your personal year is 7.

Personal year	7
Current month	8
	15

Your personal month is 6.

Personal month	6
Current day	29
	35

Your personal day for August 29, 2006 is 8.

Interpretations for Each Personal Day

Lighting the correct candle for the day is a form of single candle magic, and it enables you to make the most of what every day has to offer.

1 Personal Day

Candle: Red

A 1 personal day is a good to time to start anything new. You will have plenty of enthusiasm and energy and be receptive to new ideas. It is a good time to make a strong move forward in your career. Make something happen, and progress with it.

2 Personal Day

Candle: Orange and Silver

A 2 personal day is a time to cooperate with others, and to follow through anything begun yesterday. It is good for quiet social activities, and for close relationships. Be tactful and diplomatic, and take the day as it comes. Be patient, as nothing will happen quickly today. This is a good time for all dealings with the opposite sex.

3 Personal Day

Candle: Yellow

A 3 personal day is a good day for entertainment, fun, and pleasure. Your thoughts will be more on pleasant activities than hard work. Spend time with friends and family, and enjoy yourself. It is also a good time for creativity and all forms of self-expression.

4 Personal Day
Candle: Green and Gold
A 4 personal day is a time for hard work. It is a good time to tackle tasks that have been put off, such as household chores and visits to the dentist. Work steadily throughout the day and you'll be amazed at what you can achieve.

5 Personal Day
Candle: Blue
A 5 personal day is a time for freedom and variety. It is a good time to do something new, fresh or different, preferably something you wouldn't do normally. Expect the unexpected. It's a good time for taking a calculated risk, and for seizing hold of good opportunities.

6 Personal Day
Candle: Dark Blue or Indigo
A 6 personal day is a time for all close relationships. Family and friends are likely to play a major part today. It is a good day for domestic activities, and for artistic or creative endeavors. You may be called upon to offer help or advice. Love is favored.

7 Personal Day
Candle: Purple
A 7 personal day is a quieter time, and you are likely to want to spend at least part of the day on your own to meditate or think things through. Your spirituality and intuition are heightened at this time.

8 Personal Day

Candle: Maroon, Rose or Pink

An 8 personal day is a time to attend to business and finance. It is a day of hard work, but is also likely to be a dynamic, progressive time with a financial payoff. It is a good time for signing contracts, and for making and spending money.

9 Personal Day

Candle: All Colors, White

A 9 personal day is a good time for finishing things off, and for planning future moves. It is a good time to eliminate anything that you are completely finished with. Do not hang on to anything just for the sake of it. Your emotions are likely to be heightened, so think before speaking. Creative activities are favored.

How Long Does It Take for the Magic to Work?

Naturally, everyone wants quick results. Sometimes this occurs, but at other times you may start to wonder if, and when, it will happen. All magic involves utilizing the universal forces to make your desires a reality. You do this by first formulating the desire in your conscious mind, and then performing the necessary magic, which activates your subconscious mind and sends your desire out into the world. As long as you have done your part seriously and responsibly, the rest of the process is automatic. The universe will look after your request, and make it happen.

Remain patient. Keep positive. Make sure that you are formulating your request clearly. Ensure that you are not inadvertently hurting anyone else with your magic. Remain focused on your goal. You can use magic to achieve anything you set your mind on. Aim high, and remain confident that it will happen. Some goals take a short period of time to manifest, while others take a great deal longer.

You now know most of the basics. However, there are a number of additional things you can do to enhance the power and effectiveness of your magic. Adding fragrances of different sorts is one of these, and we will cover this in the next chapter.

Seven
Fragrance

Fragrances have always played an important role in magic. In ancient Egypt, the burning of incense was an important part of any ceremony. Incense is a fragrant mixture that is commonly used in magical and spiritual work, because it is believed to attract good spirits, and repel the bad. It was considered so important in ancient Egypt that only specially trained priests were allowed to make it. Frankincense was ritually burned at sunrise, myrrh at noon, and kyphi at sunset to mark the Sun God Ra's journey across the sky. The quality of the incenses made by the ancient Egyptians was so remarkable that Howard Carter and Lord Carnarvon were able to detect the scent in the tomb of King Tutankhamen when they entered it in 1922.[1]

The ancient Greeks believed that sending pleasant odors to the gods pleased them and made them more receptive to their requests. It is possible that the famous Oracle of Delphi used some form of incense to help her enter into an altered state. Pythia, the priestess, chewed laurel leaves and inhaled smoke fumes, which had a hypnotic effect on her.

In ancient Rome, important rituals were not considered complete until an offering of incense and frankincense had been made. Incense was also offered to the household gods, and was used in blood sacrifices. When the Christians were being persecuted by Emperor Decius (c. 200–251 CE), people who renounced their faith had to burn a few grains of incense on an altar, to prove their loyalty to the state.[2]

Medieval magicians always had their suffumigations, or correct incense, when they were performing magic. They believed that elemental spirits could use the smoke from the incense to expand and materialize.

It took the Christian Church three hundred years to start using incense in their services. Prior to this, incense was considered pagan by the church. The Jewish people had been using incense for thousands of years, and it is possible that the early Christians deliberately avoided using it to establish another point of difference between Christianity and Judaism.

Incense has been used for a number of purposes. Obviously, it is used to indicate devotion toward a particular deity. However, it can also clear the mind and allow the person to focus on his or her goal. It can be used as a stimulant and intoxicant. Most people find it relaxing, and its healing properties have been utilized by shamans all around the world. For religious purposes, it was believed that sweet-smelling incense would please the gods. Naturally, its perfume masked the unpleasant odors created with blood sacrifices. It was also believed that prayers would be wafted to heaven on the sweet-smelling smoke. In the Catholic Church, the quality of the incense being burned reflects the seniority and status of the individual.

I enjoy using incense because the pleasant perfume cleanses the air, and provides an atmosphere of sanctity, which helps me with my magic. The rising smoke symbolizes my magic reaching out to the universe.

There are three main forms of incense: loose, cone, and joss stick. Many people prefer to make their own incense, but it is readily available at specialty stores. Stick incense is the most popular, because it is economical, needs no special equipment, and burns for a long time. It can also be put out and relit when required. Loose incense is the easiest to make, but has to be burned with charcoal, which gives off soot and smoke. At one time I used mainly cone incense, but have used nothing but stick incense for many years, purely because of its convenience. Initially, the range of perfumes was limited, but that is no longer a problem. Make sure that the incense you buy is of good quality. Incense made with a gum, resin, or wood base will give you the best results.

The addition of fragrances to your magic can begin long before the ritual. It is a good idea to have a bath before engaging in any magical practice. This is a symbolic cleansing, which is made even more pleasant when selected herbs are added to the bath. You might choose hyssop, for instance, which is famed for its cleansing properties. Cedar is calming, and is another possibility. A few drops of an essential oil added to the bath is extremely effective. You might prefer to burn a pleasant-smelling oil in the room while you bathe. Alternatively, you might choose pleasant-smelling bath salts, simply because you enjoy their fragrance. Anything that smells pleasant and makes you feel good is acceptable.

After the bath, you can anoint yourself with oil, if desired. The traditional places for this are to place a spot of oil on the forehead, heart, wrists, immediately above the genitals, knees, and feet. An essential oil is perfect for this, but again, anything that smells pleasing to you will work. Remember that oils are absorbed through the skin. Consequently, you should use essential oils sparingly when anointing yourself, because they can burn.

Just as performing your magic on the right day, at the right time, increases its effectiveness, so does using the correct planetary perfumes. There are specific perfumes for each of the planets:

Sun: Acacia, amber, angelica, bay, bergamot, cassia, cinnamon, frankincense, ginger, heliotrope,

lemon, marigold, marjoram, musk, myrrh,
orange, patchouli, rosemary, saffron, sunflower

Moon: Aloe, amber, ash, camphor, cedar,
church incense, damiana, hibiscus, iris, jasmine,
juniper, lily, myrtle, peppermint, poppy, rose,
rosemary, willow, wintergreen, witch-hazel,
Ylang ylang

Mars: Basil, bay, cedar, cinnamon, coriander,
geranium, ginger, honeysuckle, menthol, musk,
opoponax, rue, sarsaparilla, tarragon, turmeric,
woodruff, wormwood

Mercury: Aniseed, basil, caraway, cassia,
cinnamon, cloves, dill, hazel, lavender, lemon,
lilac, marjoram, nutmeg, peppermint, sage,
sandalwood, vervain

Jupiter: Agrimony, aloe, ash, balm of Gilead, cedar,
cloves, copal, eucalyptus, frankincense, hyssop,
juniper, lavender, lilac, lime, marjoram, myrrh,
oak, patchouli, saffron, sandalwood

Venus: Allspice, almond, ash, catnip, cherry,
damiana, dogwood, geranium, iris, jasmine,
lavender, lemon verbena, mugwort, musk,
myrtle, nutmeg, pennyroyal, primrose, rose,
thyme, valerian, violet

Saturn: Aniseed, church incense, civet, comfrey,
cypress, ivy, musk, myrrh, oak, pine, poppy, rue,
sassafras, spikenard, vetivert, willow, wintergreen, yarrow, yew

These are simply suggestions. You can use any perfume that appeals to you, or you may prefer to conduct your magic without using perfumes at all. The ceremony needs to feel right for you. Incense adds atmosphere and helps create the right mood for many people. If you like incense, use plenty of it, as it will help your magic. If you do not enjoy the scent of incense, or can not use it for some reason, conduct your magic without it. This will not affect the ultimate result, as your intention and focus are the most important aspect of any sort of magic. This will make your magic work, with or without the use of incense. One of the best magicians I know is a chronic asthmatic, who would possibly have an attack if exposed to incense. Her magic works extremely well, showing that although it is helpful for most people, it is not essential.

In his famous book *The Magus*, published in 1801, Francis Barrett had definite views on which "fumes" should be used on different occasions. He suggested "that, according to the opinion of all magicians, in every good matter (as love, good-will, etc.), there must be a good perfume, odoriferous and precious; . . . and in evil matters (as in hatred, anger, misery, and the like), there must be made a stinking fume that is of no worth."[3] The thought of a "stinking fume" is a good deterrent.

This book is on positive, or white, magic. I hope that you will not be tempted to undertake any evil matters, as everything you do, good or bad, has a consequence. This is the universal karmic law of cause and effect. In his Epistle to the Galatians, St. Paul wrote what could be considered the essence of the law of karma: "whatsoever a man soweth, that shall he also reap" (Galatians 6:7).

It is important to remain aware of this when performing any type of magic. Self-knowledge is also vitally important, and numerology is an effective way of gaining insight into your deepest desires and motivations. Numerology also works extremely well with candle magic, which is why it is covered in the next chapter.

Eight

Numerology and Candles

Numerology is the ancient art of determining a person's personality and destiny from his or her date of birth, and full name at birth. Numerology originated in China many thousands of years go, and quickly spread around the globe. It was modernized by Pythagoras 2,600 years ago.

Numerology works very well with candle magic. No one is perfect, and our weaknesses are clearly revealed in numerology. We can then use candle magic to help rectify these problems, which makes our paths through life easier and happier.

There are four main numbers in numerology:

- Your Life Path represents 40 percent of your makeup

- Your Expression represents 30 percent of your makeup

- Your Soul Urge represents 20 percent of your makeup

- Your Day of Birth represents 10 percent of your makeup

Life Path

Your Life Path represents your purpose in life. It is determined by your date of birth. There are eleven possibilities: numbers one to nine, plus eleven and twenty-two. These last two are called Master numbers, and indicate that the person is an old soul. In other words, they have lived before in many previous incarnations, and have already learned the easier lessons. In this lifetime, they are given the opportunity to progress much further.

You work out your Life Path number by making a sum of your date of birth. This is exactly the same as the math we did to work out our cosmic vibration. We will use July 12, 1973 as an example:

Month	7
Day	12
Year	1973
	1992

We now reduce this to a single digit. We start by adding 1 + 9 + 9 + 2 = 21. We then add 2 + 1 = 3. This person has a Life Path of 3.

Here is another example, this time for someone who has a Master number for his or her Life Path.

Month	2
Day of birth	27
Year	1989
	2018

and 2 + 0 + 1 + 8 = 11. Because this is a Master number, we do not reduce it down to a single digit.

Here is another example:

Month	2
Day	29
Year	1944
	1975

and 1 + 9 + 7 + 5 = 22.

The math needs to be done in the form of a sum, as sometimes Master numbers can be lost when you add the date of birth up in a line. This is what happens to the previous date of birth when we add it up this way:

2 (month) + 2 + 9 (day) + 1 + 9 + 4 + 4 = 31, and 3 + 1 = 4.

Every Life Path has a purpose.

1 (Red)

People on a 1 Life Path have to learn to stand on their own two feet and achieve independence. Once they have done this they can become leaders, controllers, directors, and creators. People on this life path are determined, self-centered, and have to learn through their own mistakes. It can sometimes be lonely being a leader, and people on this life path will every now and again find themselves shouldering the burdens of others as well as their own.

2 (Orange)

People on a 2 Life Path are harmonious, adaptable, caring, tactful, cooperative, and diplomatic. They are sensitive, intuitive, and express their feelings well. They work well in the number two position, and make excellent go-betweens and peace makers. They rarely receive full credit for their contributions as they tend to hold themselves back, preferring to avoid the limelight.

3 (Yellow)

People on a 3 Life Path need to learn to express themselves, ideally creatively. They are light-hearted, friendly, sociable people who enjoy conversation and new ideas. They have a tendency to skim over the surface of things, reveling in new ideas, but rarely following them through. Their greatest satisfactions and rewards come when they find and develop their creative talents, which are exceptional.

4 (Green)

People on a 4 Life Path need to learn the value of hard work, discipline, and system and order. These people become involved in practical fields, and are well-organized, reliable, patient, and dependable. They like to build a firm foundation before proceeding. They are always aware of limitations and restrictions, and must learn to work within these restraints to grow and develop.

5 (Blue)

People on a 5 Life Path need to learn how to handle freedom and variety in a constructive way. People on this life path are frequently multi-talented, and choosing the right field is seldom easy because of the number of choices at their disposal. They are enthusiastic, versatile, restless, impatient people who love change, which is fortunate as they experience their full share of change and variety.

6 (Indigo)

People on a 6 Life Path need to learn home and family responsibilities. They are natural humanitarians who generally find themselves responsible for much more than their fair share. They are loving, caring people who make friends easily. They are able to balance inharmonious situations in a quiet, efficient manner. They are usually creative, and often possess a talent for music.

7 (Violet)

People on a 7 Life Path need to learn spirituality. These people grow in knowledge and wisdom as they progress through life. They need plenty of time on their own to meditate, analyze, and understand. They generally build up a strong philosophy of life. They are self-contained and need to learn trust and adaptability.

8 (Pink)

People on an 8 Life Path need to learn material freedom. They are involved in practical fields and enjoy the rewards that come from their hard work. They are ambitious, energetic, stubborn, and pragmatic. They are concerned with status and desire the best of everything.

9 (Bronze)

People on a 9 Life Path need to learn humanitarianism. Their greatest pleasures come from giving of themselves, and they usually receive little back in return. They are sociable, idealistic, supportive, and sensitive. They are more concerned with humanity as a whole than with individuals. People on this life path have a good imagination and a creative talent. It often takes them many years to find out how to use their creative gifts.

11 (Silver)

People on an 11 Life Path need to learn how to harness the added perceptions and potential that a Master number provides. This creates a degree of nervous tension that frequently works against these people's interests. Everyone except themselves is likely to be aware of their tremendous potential. They are idealistic, impractical dreamers who need to analyze and evaluate their thoughts carefully before acting. They need to learn to trust their intuition.

22 (*Gold*)

People on a 22 Life Path need to learn how to harness the nervous tension around them and achieve something big and worthwhile. Once they become aware of their enormous potential and become involved in something that challenges them, success is assured. These people are unorthodox, unconventional, and frequently charismatic.

Expression

Your expression number reveals your natural abilities. This number is derived from all the letters of your full name at birth, turned into numbers, and reduced to a single digit (or Master number). The letters are turned into numbers using a chart in which A is 1, B is 2, and so on until we reach I, which is 9. J then becomes 1 again, and the cycle continues:

1	2	3	4	5	6	7	8	9
A	B	C	D	E	F	G	H	I
J	K	L	M	N	O	P	Q	R
S	T	U	V	W	X	Y	Z	

Let's use Tom Jones as an example. When he was born, his parents named him Thomas Wilberforce Jones. He has always hated the name Wilberforce, but it is still used in determining his Expression number. Likewise, he has never been called Thomas, but we use that, rather than Tom, in determining this number.

```
THOMAS  WILBERFORCE  JONES
286411  59325966935  16551
   22         62/8       18/9
```

22 + 8 + 9 = 39, and 3 + 9 = 12. 1 + 2 = 3. Tom has an Expression number of 3.

If you look at number 3 in the interpretations of the numbers given for the Life Path, you will see what Tom is naturally good at. Tom is likely to be outgoing, sociable, and a good conversationalist. He will have good taste, and probably has a creative talent of some sort.

Here is another example. Jan Felgrew was named Janice Davina Miller at birth. Despite changing her surname when she got married, and the fact that she is always known as Jan, we use her full name at birth to determine her Expression.

```
JANICE  DAVINA  MILLER
115935  414951  493359
 24/6     24/6    33/6
```

6 + 6 + 6 = 18, and 1 + 8 = 9. Jan's Expression number is 9.

Again, if we look at the list of meanings, we find that Jan is naturally good at helping others. She is supportive, nurturing, generous, and kind-hearted.

Soul Urge

The Soul Urge reveals your inner motivations. Many people find it hard to recognize this number in themselves, as it acts as a hidden motivating force in their lives. It can be extremely helpful to know what this number is, as you can then harness the energies of your Soul Urge to enable you to achieve your goals (number values are the same as in the expression chart, page 97).

The Soul Urge is derived from the vowels of the person's full name at birth, reduced to a single digit (or Master number). To complicate this, Y is frequently classed as a vowel. When Y acts as a vowel (as in the names Yvonne, Mervyn, and Harry), it is classed as a vowel. If the Y follows another vowel and is not pronounced separately (as in Kaye, Hayden and Beythe), it is also classed as a vowel.

Here is an example:

```
DONNA   MARIE   CARMODY
   6      1    1 95    1    6 7
          7      15/6           14/5
```

7 + 6 + 5 = 18, and 1 + 8 = 9. Donna's Soul Urge is 9. This means that she is motivated to help people, and wants to share her creativity with others.

Here is another example:

HAYDEN MCINEARNY JOHNSON
  17 5   9 51 7 6   6
  13/4   22   12/3

4 + 22 + 3 = 29, and 2 + 9 = 11. Hayden's Soul Urge is 11. This means that he is motivated to share his idealistic view of life with others. He is likely to be a gifted dreamer, who visualizes himself helping humanity in some sort of way.

Day of Birth

The Day of Birth number is the person's day of birth reduced down to a single digit, or a Master number. The Master number days of birth are the 11th, 22nd, and 29th of any month.

Your day of birth is the final 10 percent of your makeup, and it has an influence on the other numbers. Here is an example. Someone born on the 9th of any month would have a 9 day of birth. This would soften the more aggressive approach this person would have if his or her Life Path was a 1. If these numbers were reversed, and the person had a 9 Life Path, the 1 day of birth would ensure that he or she looked after his or her own needs, along with those of everyone else.

How to Use Your Numerology Colors

It is possible that two or more of the four colors in your numerological makeup are the same. Consequently, you will have one, two, three, or four different colors that represent you. You can use any, or all, of these colors to represent you in any form of candle magic.

If your magic involves your purpose in life, you would choose a candle that represented your Life Path. If your magic was concerned with developing or improving your natural abilities you would use the color that represented your Expression. Finally, if your magic was concerned with your innermost desires you would use the color that represented your Soul Urge.

Self-Nurturing Exercise

Everyone needs to nurture themselves now and again. When you feel good about yourself, you can achieve virtually anything. Lack of self-worth is a major failing of humanity. This brief self-nurturing exercise will raise your self-esteem, and enable you to achieve much more than you ever thought possible.

You need four candles to represent your four main numerological numbers. It makes no difference if two or more of the colors are the same. Let's assume that your numbers are: Life Path 1, Expression 1, Soul Urge 5, and Day of birth 4. This means that you would need two red candles, one blue candle, and one green candle.

Place these in a row on an altar or table. The candle that represents your Life Path should be on your left as you look at the row, and the Day of birth candle should be on the right. Light all four candles and sit down in a

comfortable chair facing them. Watch the flames flickering, but do not focus on any particular candle. Think
about your life in general terms. You may want to think
about aspects of your past. You may prefer to look forward
and think about your hopes and dreams. Allow your mind
to drift and think about any aspect of your life that you
wish. Gradually, you will start thinking about the matters
that are important to you at the present moment. As you
gaze at the candle, think about the current situation and
allow yourself to drift forward into the future, seeing yourself, in your imagination, confident, strong, and able to
achieve anything. Hold this thought for as long as you
can. When your mind starts to drift again, put out the
candles, starting with the Day of Birth one, followed by
the Soul Urge, Expression, and finally Life Path.

Once this small ritual is over, you will find yourself
carrying on with your everyday life in a calm and relaxed
manner, feeling confident and sure of yourself. Repeat
this self-nurturing ritual as often as you wish. You can do
it whenever you feel the need for it. If you are lacking in
confidence, or have an important goal you are aiming for,
do this ritual every day. If life is going pretty much the
way you want it to be, perform this exercise once a week.
You cannot do it too often.

Ultimate Purpose Exercise

You will need a candle that represents your Life Path for
this exercise. Choose the most attractive looking candle
that you can find. Place it on a table, and sit down on an

upright chair, with your arms resting on the tabletop, and your hands on each side of the candle.

Sit for a few moments, contemplating the unlit candle. It symbolizes you, as you are now. The unlit candle symbolizes your potential, and what you are capable of achieving. Close your eyes for a few moments and think about your life's purpose. Look back over your life, and then project yourself forward to see what your life will be like when you are fully on track.

When you feel ready, light the candle, and encircle it with your hands. Take a few deep breaths, and exhale slowly. Stare at the flame, and imagine the smoke going out into the universe to summon to you whatever it is you need to fulfill your purpose in this lifetime.

Close your eyes for a few moments, and visualize yourself as you are going to be once you achieve your purpose. Wait until you feel a sense of confidence and acceptance inside you. This shows that your inner being is prepared to help you achieve your purpose.

Open your eyes and stare at the flame for a minute or two. Ask for any guidance, protection, or wisdom that you feel you might need. If you are not certain of how to fulfill your life's purpose, ask for help now. I prefer to say the words out loud, but you can ask for help silently, if you prefer.

Say "thank you" three times, snuff out the candle, and stand up to stretch. Write down in a diary or notebook any insights that occurred to you as you performed this exercise.

Use this candle solely for this particular exercise. Each time you do it new insights will come to you. This is why it is important to write down your feelings about the exercise as soon as it is over.

Developing Your Potential Exercise

You need a candle to symbolize your Expression number for this exercise. Sit at a table, with the candle in front of you, in the same manner as in the Ultimate Purpose exercise. Close your eyes and think of your many talents and skills. I know many people who think they have no special talents, but this is not the case. Everyone is good at something. You might be a good listener, for instance. You might have an empathy with young or old people. Your skills and talents do not need to be related to sports or intellectual pursuits. Surely it is better to be a good, kind, loving person than be able to run one hundred yards in under ten seconds.

This is not a time for modesty. No one will know what you are thinking about it. Go over your different skills one by one, and decide on the particular talent you wish to develop further.

Once it is clear in your mind, open your eyes and light the candle. Encircle the candle with your hands. You can hold the candle, if you prefer. Think of the talent you wish to develop as you stare at the flame. Think of your desire going out into the universe, and visualize everything you need to achieve it coming back to you. Picture yourself as you will be once this talent has been developed.

Ask for any help you may need in accomplishing your goal. A friend of mine asked for a new violin teacher, and met the perfect person just two days later.

Gaze into the flame and say "thank you" three times, then snuff out the flame. Stand up, stretch, and write down any insights that came to you as you performed the experiment.

Motivation Exercise

This exercise is similar to the two preceding ones. However, it should not be done until after you have received some insight from them. You need a candle that symbolizes your Soul Urge.

Sit down comfortably and light the candle. Stare at the flame and silently ask for the necessary motivation to help you attain your goals. Remind yourself that you have unlimited potential, and that you can achieve anything you set your mind on. I find it helpful to say out loud, "I have unlimited potential." I repeat these words until I feel a wave of enthusiasm and energy sweep through me, confirming the truth in those words.

Once you have reached this stage, say out loud: "I will achieve (this goal). I deserve it, and am prepared to do whatever it takes to achieve it. I thank you (whatever deity you wish) for enabling me to achieve this goal."

Stare into the flame for another minute or two. When you feel the time is right, say "thank you" three times, and snuff the candle out. Stand up, stretch, and carry on with your day, confident that you will achieve your goal.

Karmic Factors

Karma is the law of cause and effect. It is completely impartial. Some people associate it with retribution and punishment, but this is not the case. All it means is that everything balances out eventually. If you do a good deed today, you will build up karmic credits as a result. Equally, if you do something bad, you will ultimately pay back the negative karma that you created. The average person is creating positive and negative karma all the time.

It is a simple matter to determine what, if any, unresolved karmic factors apply in your relationships. This occurs only if you share the first vowel in your first name at birth with anyone who is close to you. For example, my first name is Richard. If I was involved with someone called Hillary, Ivy, Philippa, or anyone else who had an I as the first vowel, there would be a karmic element in our relationship that dated from a previous lifetime.

If Sandy became involved with David there would be an unresolved karmic element in their relationship. However, there would be no unresolved karma in her relationship if she settled down with Douglas, Henry, or William. She may have shared a previous lifetime with Douglas, Henry or William, but any karma created was resolved before this present incarnation.

Obviously, there are karmic factors involved only in close, ongoing relationships. There is unlikely to be a karmic element if your name is Janet and you happen to work with someone called Jason.

People tend to think that karmic factors dating from a previous lifetime are always bad. This is not necessarily the case. If a couple had a joyful, happy previous life together, they may have come back together in this lifetime to develop their bonds of love even further. This is especially the case if they both have the same Soul Urge number. These people exist solely for each other, and are the most fortunate of people.

Anything worthwhile takes a great deal of hard work, and these people would have worked hard at their relationships in previous lifetimes, as well as this one, to reach this stage.

Karmic relationships are learning experiences, and the two people are brought together in this lifetime to resolve issues that were not rectified in a previous life. Unfortunately, this is not usually an easy matter. However, candle magic can play a part in easing troubled karmic relationships, and allow the couple to work through their difficulties.

You need a candle to represent the two people involved. The simplest way is to use basic correspondences:

A = red
E = blue
I = bronze
O = indigo
U = yellow
Y = violet

Planetary Rulers of the Vowels

If you prefer, you can use the colors that are related to the planetary rulers of the vowels:

A = Mars = Red
E = Venus = Green
I = Saturn = Black
O = Jupiter = Blue
U = Moon = White
Y = Mercury = Orange

Karmic Factors Exercise

You need two candles of the same color to symbolize you and your partner. Place these on opposite sides of a table. Light them both and then sit down on an upright chair between them. Look straight ahead, so that you can see the flames of both candles with your peripheral vision. Think about your relationship and how valuable it is to you. Accept the fact that because it is a karmic relationship it is not likely to be easy, but will enable both of you to learn and grow immeasurably in this incarnation. Think about some of the happy times you shared together. Think of the time you met, and what you saw in him or her. Think how much you want the relationship to continue to grow and develop.

Pause and move each candle a few inches nearer the center of the table.

Continue to look between the two candles and think in general terms about your relationship. Say out loud: "I want our relationship to work." Move each candle another few inches toward the center of the table.

Think about the future, and how much you want your relationship to grow and develop. Say out loud: "I want our relationship to last." Move the candles again.

Keep on doing this, thinking about your relationship, and gradually moving the candles closer and closer to each other until they are touching. When they finally touch, encircle them with your hands, close your eyes for a few seconds, and say: "Thank you, thank you, thank you."

Snuff out the candles, take several deep breaths, and allow the universe to work on your difficulties. Put the candles away carefully. Keep on doing this exercise at regular intervals until the candles have been fully burned.

It is believed that numerology began when Wu of Hsia, allegedly the first emperor of China, noticed strange markings on the shell of a tortoise, some five thousand years ago. Feng shui comes from the same source, as does the concept of five elements. As each element relates to both a direction and a color, knowledge of these can enhance your skills at candle magic. We will look at this in the next chapter.

Nine

The Five Elements

In recent years Feng shui has become extremely popular all around the world. Among other things, it has introduced Westerners to the ancient Chinese concept of the five elements. These are wood, fire, earth, metal, and water. Although they are related to the physical objects they are named after, they should be regarded as different types of energies, rather than something physical. Each element is related to a color, season, direction, and planet. Everything is symbolically made up of these five elements, and you can create harmony in your life by using and harnessing these energies. You can find your personal element in Appendix A (p. 219).

You can use the numerous associations connected with the five elements to increase the effectiveness of your candle magic. You might, for instance, use the elements to choose the correct color candle for your specific goal. You can use candle magic, along with the elements, to help you get on better with all the important people in your life. Burning the candles associated with the elements will also help you meditate, nurture yourself, reduce stress, and achieve your goals.

Wood

Wood relates to the color green, the season spring, and the direction east. If you have wood as an element you will be creative and will want to express yourself in some way. You will also be sociable and easy to get along with, although you are bound to be stubborn at times. This is because wood can be pliable and bending (willow), but also strong and unyielding (oak).

The color green has a variety of shades ranging from a deep olive green through blue-green to an almost yellow lime green.

Fire

Fire relates to the color red, the season summer, and the direction south. If your element is fire you will be full of energy and enthusiasm. However, you need to remember that although fire warms and cheers, it can also burn and destroy.

The color red ranges from a deep fire red to maroon, violet, dark purple, orangey-red, and pink.

Earth

Earth relates to the colors brown and yellow. It relates not to a direction, but the center. If earth is your element, you will be patient, honest, methodical, and hard-working. You will be easy to get along with, but rigid and fixed in outlook.

Any earth color can be used when choosing a suitable candle. These range from brown through saffron to orange and yellow.

Metal

Metal relates to the colors gold, silver, and white, the season autumn, and direction west. If your element is metal you will be involved in financial and business undertakings. Metal symbolizes harvest and success.

White and gold are the traditional colors for this element, but any metallic color can be used as well.

Water

Water relates to the colors blue and black. It represents the season winter, and direction north. If your element is water you will be interested in travel, communication, and learning. You may be involved in the arts, the media, and possibly literature.

Blue and black are the traditional colors of the water element. The blue can range from a dark blue through navy to an almost green turquoise-blue.

The elements relate to each other in different ways, and there are two cycles that illustrate this. The first is known as the Cycle of Production.

Cycle of Production

The Productive Cycle is also known as the Cycle of Birth and the Cycle of Harmony. The sequence is:

Wood – Fire – Earth – Metal – Water – Wood.

This is because wood burns, and that creates fire. From fire we get ashes, which symbolically creates earth. Metal comes from the earth, which means that earth creates metal. Metal liquefies, which symbolically creates water. Finally, water nurtures and creates wood.

This never-ending cycle shows how each element nurtures and sustains the element that follows it in the cycle. Wood, for instance, helps fire. Fire helps earth, and so on.

This cycle can be looked at in reverse. This is known as the Cycle of Reduction. Each element in this cycle has a calming and soothing effect on the element that precedes it in the cycle.

Consequently, the element that precedes your element in the Productive Cycle nurtures and sustains you, and the element that follows you in the series soothes and calms you. If your element is metal, for example, you are nurtured by earth, and calmed by water. Wood is nurtured by water and calmed by fire.

Cycle of Destruction

The Destructive Cycle is the opposite in effect to the Productive Cycle, and has the following sequence:

Fire – Metal – Wood – Earth – Water – Fire

In this sequence, fire melts metal. Metal chops down wood. Wood drains from the earth. Earth drains water, and water puts out fire.

We can use these cycles in a number of different ways:

1. If you want to meditate quietly, you can burn a candle of the color that represents your element. If you belonged to the Fire element, for example, you would burn a red candle.

2. If you want to achieve a certain goal, you can burn a candle of the color of the element that precedes yours in the Productive Cycle. If, for example, your element is Wood, you would burn a blue or black candle.

3. If you are stressed, angry, or upset, you can burn a candle that relates to the element that follows yours in the Productive cycle. If your element was Earth, for instance, you would burn a gold, silver, or white candle.

4. If you are wanting to nurture yourself, you can create a ritual using three candles: one representing your element, and one each for the

elements that precede and follow yours. If you belonged to the Metal element, for instance, you would place a gold, silver, or white candle in the center of your altar. On one side of this, you would place a yellow or brown candle (Earth element), while on the other side you would place a blue or black candle (Water element).

5. If you were having dealings with someone whose element followed yours in the Cycle of Destruction, you should determine which element comes between them in the Cycle of Production, and burn a candle of that color on your altar to neutralize any potential negativity. Let's assume that your element is Wood and you are entering into a relationship with someone from the Earth element. In the Cycle of Production, Fire is between Wood and Earth. Therefore, you would burn a red candle to symbolize the Fire element.

Self-Development

We can take this even further and use the elements to help us progress in different areas of life. If, for example, you desire more money, you should burn a candle that relates to the element that follows your element in the Cycle of Destruction. If your element is Wood, you would burn a yellow or brown candle, as Earth is the element that immediately follows Wood in this cycle.

If you desire more status, or want to raise your reputation in the community, you would benefit by burning a candle that relates to the element that immediately precedes yours in the Cycle of Destruction. If your element is Metal, you would burn a red candle, as Fire is the element that immediately precedes Metal.

If you desire more support, appreciation, and authority, you should burn a candle that relates to the element that immediately precedes yours in the Cycle of Production. If your element is Water, for instance, you would burn a gold, silver, or white candle, as Metal immediately precedes Water in the Productive Cycle.

If you are studying, or want to express yourself in some way, you should burn a candle that relates to the element that immediately follows yours in the Cycle of Production. If your element is Wood, for example, you would burn a red candle, as Fire is the element that follows Wood in the Productive Cycle.

If you are having problems with friends or colleagues you should burn a candle of the element that represents you. If you belong to the Fire element, for instance, you should burn a red candle.

People In Your Life

The important people in your life are all represented by different elements. These are not necessarily the personal elements that are related to their year of birth. These elements reveal their relationship to you. You should burn candles of the colors that relate to these elements whenever you want to help them in some way. If someone is unwell, for example, you can burn a candle of the color that relates to their element in the chart below. You can do the same if you are having difficulties with someone close to you. If someone needs motivation, courage, strength, or support, burn a candle to help them. It will send your blessings to them.

The origin of these family relationships is interesting and logical. The children of the mother, for example, are always of the element that follows hers in the Cycle of Production. This is because she gives birth to them. Likewise, her husband always belongs to the element that precedes hers in the Cycle of Destruction. This is because he traditionally conquered her. In a man's group of elements the children always belong to the element that precedes his in the Cycle of Destruction. This is because they grow up and gradually supersede him as he grows old and eventually dies. Naturally, this means that his father belongs to the element that is destroyed by his element in the Cycle of Destruction. (His father and wife are both "destroyed" by the same element.)

Wood Man

Element	Person
Wood	Self, Brothers, Sisters
Earth	Wife, Father
Metal	Children
Water	Mother

Wood Woman

Element	Person
Wood	Self, Brothers, Sisters
Earth	Father
Metal	Husband
Water	Mother
Fire	Children

Fire Man

Element	Person
Fire	Self, Brothers, Sisters
Metal	Wife, Father
Water	Children
Wood	Mother

Fire Woman

Element	Person
Fire	Self, Brothers, Sisters
Earth	Children
Metal	Father
Water	Husband
Wood	Mother

Earth Man

Element	Person
Earth	Self, Brothers, Sisters
Water	Wife, Father
Wood	Children
Fire	Mother

Earth Woman

Element	Person
Earth	Self, Brothers, Sisters
Metal	Children
Water	Father
Wood	Husband
Fire	Mother

Metal Man

Element	Person
Metal	Self, Brothers, Sisters
Wood	Wife, Father
Fire	Children
Earth	Mother

Metal Woman

Element	Person
Metal	Self, Brothers, Sisters
Water	Children
Wood	Father
Fire	Husband
Earth	Mother

Water Man

Element	Person
Water	Self, Brothers, Sisters
Fire	Wife, Father
Earth	Children
Metal	Mother

Water Woman

Element	Person
Water	Self, Brothers, Sisters
Wood	Children
Fire	Father
Earth	Husband
Metal	Mother

Experiment with the five elements. To the best of my knowledge, they have not been used with candle magic before, and you have the opportunity to perform valuable, original research. Record your results over a period of time and prove for yourself the effectiveness of the five elements when used with candle magic.

There will be times when you want to conceal what you are doing from others, or may want to add extra power to your candle magic. Using a magical alphabet can help you do both of these. This will be covered in the next chapter.

Ten
Magical Alphabets

Secret alphabets have been used in magic, and for other purposes, for thousands of years. The runes and the oghams are the best-known examples of ancient magical alphabets.

Some alphabets were devised to ensure that important information remained secret. Examples of these were the secret alphabets used by the Vehmgericht and the Inquisition. The Vehmgericht, allegedly founded in 772 CE by Emperor Charlemagne, consisted of a number of vigilante groups who acted as secret executioners. In the fifteenth century the Vehmgericht became allied with the Inquisition. To conceal their records these evil organizations devised secret alphabets based on magical ones that were in use at the time. Their alphabets are no longer used, and are of interest only to historians.[1]

Secrecy is a valid reason for using a magical alphabet. Medieval magicians usually worked alone and did not want anyone else to know their methods. Consequently, they recorded their discoveries and explorations in their grimoires using a secret alphabet. You might want to inscribe a message or a person's name on a candle for a particular purpose. For a variety of reasons, you may not want other people to know what you have written. Using a magical alphabet solves the problem.

The more usual reason for using a magical alphabet is that it forces you to concentrate on what you are doing. If, for example, you have a candle to represent a woman called Michele, you could inscribe her name in English without really thinking about it. This is because you are so used to writing in English that your hand can write the word with little conscious effort. However, the opposite occurs if you write the word in a secret alphabet. If you wrote Michele in, say, the Theban alphabet you would be forced to concentrate on every movement you made. This helps you to focus on your intent while working on the candle.

Whenever possible, when you are inscribing someone's name on a candle, try to include additional information about the person as well. This might be their zodiac sign, Ascendant, Life Path number, personal element, date of birth, nickname, character traits, favorite flower, or anything else that you know about the person. If you do not know the person's name, which is common in rituals designed to attract a partner, inscribe the candle with the characteristics you would like this person to possess.

In the past magicians often knew Greek, Latin, and Hebrew, and used these languages to keep their knowledge secret from less well-educated people. In addition to these, esoteric alphabets were devised to ensure greater secrecy. Unfortunately, most of these were passed down from magician to magician, and errors and variations have developed as a result. The derivation of most of these is not known.

However, historians have uncovered the origins of some of them. The Enochian language was discovered by the clairvoyance of Dr. John Dee, and his colleague, Edward Kelly (also spelled Kelley), and the Alphabet of the Magi was first published in 1870.[2] Cornelius Agrippa was the first person to publish a secret way of writing numbers, and also explained sacred letters and Celestial, or Angelic, writing.[3] The Angelic alphabet is still used by some ceremonial magicians today. Ceremonial magicians also use the Malachim (also known as Language of the Magi) and Passing the River alphabets.

Theban script, sometimes known as Honorian, is a popular alphabet used by many Gardnerian witches. In fact, it is sometimes known as the "Witches' Runes," which is incorrect.

Francis Barrett listed several esoteric alphabets in his book *The Magus*, published in 1801. Dozens have been published since.[4]

Some alphabets are comparatively easy to draw, while others are more difficult. I have experimented with several alphabets over the years, and find the Templar alphabet the easiest to inscribe onto the side of a candle. I have also used the ogham alphabet, and the runes.

I have included several magical alphabets in Appendix B (p. 225). Experiment and decide which ones you like. Remember to use only one alphabet in any ritual. The candles lose some of their effectiveness if one is inscribed in Theban, another in runes, and a third in ogham. In fact, it is better to choose an alphabet that you like, and use it exclusively.

You might even decide to create your own magical alphabet. I know several people who have done this. It is an interesting intellectual exercise, and you will end up with something unique and special to you. This further associates the candle to you and your magic. Bill Whitcomb has a chapter on creating your own magical alphabet in his excellent book *The Magician's Reflection*.[5]

You can inscribe the information on the candle in any way you wish. I used to use a heated knitting needle, but found that a sharp knife worked better for me. A friend of mine uses a soldering iron. It works well for him, but I had problems with melting wax when I tried to use it, and found it difficult to create attractive-looking work.

Most people write their message from the top of the candle toward the base. If the message is a single word you can draw it in a straight line. However, if the message is lengthy, inscribe it in a spiral fashion around the candle, starting at the top.

Many magicians still record their experiments using a magical alphabet. This is not as essential today, as modern-day computers allow you to hide information behind a series of passwords and other protective devices. In some ways, this is a shame, but there is no halting progress. Fortunately, magical alphabets will continue to be used as long as it is necessary to attach words to objects, such as candles, that might be seen by the uninitiated.

Magic squares, like magical alphabets, occupy a small footnote in history. Magic squares are considered to be nothing but a curiosity to mathematicians, but their influence in magic has been incredible. We will look at them in the next chapter.

Eleven

Magic Squares

Magic squares have been used in magic for thousands of years. It is believed that the first magic square was found in the markings of a tortoise shell in China. The first of the legendary pre-historical emperors was a man called Wu of Hsia (2953–2838 BCE). Before he became emperor, he was supervising irrigation works on the Yellow River. One day, while he and his men were working, a large tortoise crawled out of the river. This was considered a good omen, as people believed that gods lived inside the shells of tortoises and turtles. However, when they examined the tortoise more closely, they found a perfect magic square in the markings on the shell. Wu considered this so important that all the wise men of the day were summoned to inspect it. From this study came Chinese astrology, numerology, the I Ching, feng shui, the ki and kigaku.

A magic square is an arrangement of numbers in which every horizontal, vertical, and diagonal row adds up to the same total. The magic square on the back of the tortoise was a three-by-three square:

4	9	2
3	5	7
8	1	6

Until mathematicians became interested in them two hundred years ago, magic squares were used primarily for talismanic and divination purposes. These squares are still a major force in Asian magic, where they are known as yantras. Magic squares became popular in the Western magical tradition because of the explorations of Abbot Johannes Trithemius (1462–1516), Peter d'Abano (c.1250–c.1316), Cornelius Agrippa (c.1486–1535), and Francis Barrett (c.1774–?), who advocated using magic squares as talismans.

A magic square is called *kamea* in Hebrew. In the Kabbalah, the seven kamea are associated with the seven traditional planets on the Tree of Life. Each planet is believed to possess a spirit or mind that can guide, inspire, and direct through the kamea.

There is a kamea, or magic square, for each day of the week. This allows you to perform candle magic every day, if you wish. At its most basic, all that is required is that you draw the magic square for whichever day of the week it is, and burn it in a candle of the correct color. Naturally, there is more to it than that, and ideally, you should create a formalized ritual to ensure that you receive all the benefits that are due to you.

All of these rituals use just one candle.

Sunday

Start by drawing the magic square of the Sun on a sheet of good quality paper. I like to do this on my altar. I also place a gold candle in the center.

6	32	3	34	35	1
7	11	27	28	8	30
19	14	16	15	23	24
18	20	22	21	17	13
25	29	10	9	26	12
35	5	33	4	2	31

Take your time, and make the magic square as neat as possible. While you are constructing it, think pleasant thoughts about universal peace, love, and kindness. The kamea of the Sun is also good for hopes, prospects, increase, and friendship.

When you are finished, light the candle and place the magic square on your altar in front of it. Sit down and gaze at the gold candle. Think about the richness of the color gold, and how it has always been related to the Sun. Think about a perfect world, and how different life would be if people stopped bickering and got along with each other.

Consciously relax your body, paying special attention to areas that seem tense. When you feel totally relaxed, give thanks to God, the universal life force, or whichever deity you prefer, for all the blessings in your life.

Pick up the magic square and place it on your right palm. Rest the back of your right hand on your left palm. Stand up and slowly raise both hands until they are about chest height. Speak to the magic square. "I offer you to the universal forces to help create peace and understanding throughout the world. I offer you with my blessing." If you are using this kamea for financial purposes, and there is no reason why you should not, add: "I ask for a blessing on all my endeavors and trust that you will grant me prosperity and happiness."

Pause for a few moments, and then burn the sheet of paper in the candle flame. You might want to hold the paper with a pair of tongs to avoid the risk of burning yourself. I normally hold it by one corner, and let this drop into the flame when it gets too hot to hold any longer.

Once the magic square has completely disappeared, give thanks to the universe for allowing your desires to go out into the world. Snuff out the candle, and carry on with your day.

I have special candles that I use for magic square candle magic. After each ritual, I put them away carefully, so that they can be used again a week later.

Monday

Monday is a good day to work on developing your intuition. It is also good for travel and matters relating to love and romance. Draw the magic square of Luna on a sheet of good quality paper. Think of how useful your psychic and intuitive capabilities are to you, and how you would like to continue to develop these gifts.

37	78	29	70	21	62	13	54	5
6	38	79	30	71	22	63	14	46
47	7	39	80	31	72	23	55	15
16	48	8	40	81	32	64	24	56
57	17	49	9	41	73	33	65	25
26	58	18	50	1	42	74	34	66
67	27	59	10	51	2	43	75	35
36	68	19	60	11	52	3	44	76
77	28	69	20	61	12	53	4	45

You will also need a silver candle. Place this in the center of your altar, and put the magic square in front of it.

Light the candle, and sit down comfortably. Gaze at the candle, and think about the hidden, mysterious aspects of life. Think of occasions when your intuition helped you. It doesn't matter how large or small these moments may have been.

Relax your body, and give thanks to whichever deity you prefer for the blessings in your life. Ask for help in developing your intuition. When you feel ready, stand up, pick up the magic square, hold it at chest height for a few moments and speak to it. "I offer you to the universal forces as a small token of thanks for your help in enabling me to develop my psychic awareness. Please help me take this to the next level. Thank you." If you wish, you can add words relating to travel or love.

Burn the magic square in the flame. Give thanks to the universal forces for allowing you to send your desire out into the world. Snuff out the candle and carry on with your day.

Tuesday

The kamea or magic square of Mars represents Tuesday. This is a good day to work on your enthusiasm, drive, leadership capabilities, courage, confidence, health, and vitality.

11	24	7	20	3
4	12	25	8	16
17	5	13	21	9
10	18	1	14	22
23	6	19	2	15

While you are constructing it, think of your need for more confidence, energy, health, and drive.

Place a red candle in the center of your altar and rest your magic square in front of it. Light the candle and sit down comfortably where you can gaze at the flame. Think about your life in general terms. Think of the moments when you felt your confidence let you down, or you failed to do the best you could. Think of other occasions when you were full of energy, enthusiasm, confidence, and vibrant health. Decide what you want for the future. As you look at the candle, think about all the positive qualities of red, the color of Tuesday's candle.

Relax your body, and think of all the good things about your life. Ponder the fact that you are you, are alive, have considerable talents and abilities, and enormous potential. Realize that you can, in fact, achieve anything at all that you set your mind on.

Stand up, and hold the magic square at chest height. Speak to whichever deity you wish. "I thank you for all the blessings in my life, for my family, friends, career, and talents. I also ask you to give me more (enthusiasm, confidence, self-esteem, good health, etc.). Thank you."

When you feel ready, burn the magic square. Thank the universal forces for allowing you to send your request out into the world. Snuff out the candle, and carry on with your day, confident that you have taken a major step toward becoming the person you want to be.

Wednesday

You will need a yellow candle and the kamea of Mercury to perform this ritual.

8	58	59	5	4	62	63	1
49	15	14	52	53	11	10	56
41	23	22	44	45	19	18	48
32	34	35	29	28	38	39	25
40	26	27	37	36	30	31	33
17	47	46	20	21	43	42	24
9	55	54	12	13	51	50	16
64	2	3	61	60	6	7	57

While you are constructing this kamea, think about your brain, mind, intellect, and mental capabilities. The kamea of Mercury is also good for eloquence and business matters. Place the finished kamea on your altar in front of the yellow candle. Light the candle and sit down comfortably where you can gaze at it. Think of the qualities of yellow, and then allow your mind to think about your wonderful brain, your ability to learn and gain knowledge, and your amazing memory. Although, like everyone else, you forget things at times, your mind remembers everything—it's just the recall that is sometimes faulty. Once you have the information, you are able to impart this knowledge to others, enriching their lives in the process.

Relax your body and give thanks to the almighty for your mind and powerful intellect. When you feel ready, stand up and hold the magic square at chest height. Speak out loud to whichever deity you prefer. "Thank you for equipping me with my intelligence, powers of speech, reason, and understanding. I am grateful for my memory, logical mind, and powers of comprehension. Please help me develop all of these gifts further, so that I can make the most of every moment in this incarnation. Thank you." If you are involved in business matters, you may want to add: "Please help me develop my business skills so that I can achieve success in my field. I want to be fair and honest to all, and also desire a worthwhile return on my efforts and investment."

Pause for several seconds and then burn the magic square. Thank the universal forces for making it possible for you to send your request out to the universe. When you feel ready, snuff out the candle and carry on with your day.

Thursday

The kamea of Jupiter is the magic square for Thursday. You will need this, and a green candle, to perform this ritual.

4	14	15	1
9	7	6	12
5	11	10	8
16	2	3	13

Jupiter is related to expansion and success, especially financial increase. However, it includes abundance in all areas of life, including friendships and health. Think about these things as you construct the kamea of Jupiter. Place the green candle in the center of your altar, with the magic square resting on the table in front of it.

Light the candle and sit down facing it. Think about the different blessings in your life, and give thanks for them. Think of the things you would like to have more abundantly in your life. Think of the changes that would occur in your life if you had more money, for instance. Think about better health, if you are unwell. Think about the people you know and how your life could be enriched with more good friends.

Relax as much as you can, and allow feelings of abundance to sweep over and through your body. Enjoy these feelings for as long as you can.

When you feel ready, stand up and hold the magic square at chest level. Give thanks to whichever deity you wish. "Thank you for all the blessings in my life. I feel truly fortunate, and am very grateful. However, I feel I would benefit by having more financial security. This would allow me to (buy a house, feed my family, give money to the poor, etc.). Please enable me to achieve my financial goals so I can help my self, my family, and others. Thank you." Naturally, this should be changed to reflect your desires. If you want more friends, ask for them. Request perfect health, if that is what you need.

Pause until you feel the moment is right, and then burn the kamea of Jupiter. Thank the universal forces for listening to your request, snuff out the candle, and carry on with your day.

Friday

The kamea of Venus is the magic square for Friday. You will also need a pink candle.

22	47	16	41	10	35	4
5	23	48	17	42	11	29
30	6	24	49	18	36	12
13	31	7	25	43	19	37
38	14	32	1	26	44	20
21	39	8	33	2	27	45
46	15	40	9	34	3	28

While you are constructing the kamea, think pleasant thoughts about love, romance, harmony, friendship, and beauty. Place the finished magic square on your altar in front of the pink candle.

Light the candle and sit down in front of it, watching the flame as it dances and flickers. Think about the important role love and romance has in your life. Think about lost opportunities, as well as successful romantic encounters. If there is a special person in your life, think loving thoughts about him or her.

Relax your body as much as possible, and try to recapture the feelings you had in the past when you knew you were in love. When you feel ready, stand up and hold the kamea at chest level. Talk to whichever deity you wish. "Thank you for giving me the gifts of love and passion, and for all the beauty and joy there is in my life. I am grateful for all of these bounties. Please grant me (a new partner, a soul mate, more passion, more beauty, new friends, pleasant activities, etc.). Thank you."

Wait a minute or two, and see if you receive a response. It might be a feeling of exultation that sweeps through and over you. It might simply be a sense of knowing, or a feeling of peace. When you feel ready, burn the magic square. Thank the universal forces for listening to you, and for granting your request. Snuff out the candle, and return to your everyday life.

Saturday

The kamea for Saturday is one you will be familiar with,

as it is the same magic square that was found in the markings of a tortoise's shell almost five thousand years ago.

$$
\begin{array}{ccc}
4 & 9 & 2 \\
3 & 5 & 7 \\
8 & 1 & 6
\end{array}
$$

You will also need a dark blue candle. Saturn relates to patience, determination, persistence, understanding and discipline. Think about these things as you construct the kamea. When it is finished, place it on your altar in front of the blue candle. Light the candle and sit down comfortably.

Gaze at the candle and think about times when you were patient and understanding, and other occasions when you weren't. Think of your need for self-discipline, for hard work and determination, for patience and understanding. You will need all of these things to help you achieve your goals.

Relax as much as you can, and think about times in the past when you achieved a difficult or challenging goal. Try to recapture the feelings you had then.

When you feel ready, stand up in front of your altar and hold the magic square at chest height. As on the other days, speak to whichever deity you wish. "Thank you for helping me get to this stage in my life. I am grateful to you for your patience and understanding, especially at times when I lacked it myself. Please help me develop the qualities I need to achieve my purpose in this lifetime. I am prepared to do whatever is necessary to achieve this goal. Thank you for your love, understanding, compassion, and help."

Pause for several seconds and then burn the magic square in the flame. Thank the universal forces once again for helping you to achieve all that you desire, snuff out the candle, and carry on with your day, confident that your desires will become a reality.

You will receive a great deal of pleasure by performing these rituals on a regular basis. The rituals are all simple, and can be done in about ten minutes. Do not rush them, however. Sometimes you might need ten minutes, while on another occasion the same ritual may take three or four times as long. Do not expect miracles the first time you perform these rituals. Repeating them over and over again provides enormous power and energy that can propel you to enormous success. However, time, repetition, and patience are all required. Nothing worthwhile happens without enthusiasm, intent, and effort.

As the combination of candles and magic squares shows, you can use candle magic for almost any purpose. However, we have not yet discussed one of the most important aspects of candle magic: healing. It would be hard to imagine anything more worthwhile than this. Consequently, healing with candles is the subject of the next chapter.

Twelve

Healing with Candles

Magic should be used to help others. It would be hard to find anything more important than helping someone who is unwell. Candle burning should be considered complementary to normal health care, rather than an alternative. Naturally, anyone who is unwell should consult their health professional, but candle burning can help by sending healing vibrations to the sick person.

You can also use candle healing to help yourself, both when you are physically ill, and when you are emotionally unwell.

Healing Meditation

Color healing has helped many people restore their minds, bodies, and souls. Every color puts out its own unique energy which affects us in many different ways. We can take advantage of this when performing a candle meditation.

You will need several candles of different colors. However, only one is used during the meditation. Choose a candle that seems to be right for you at the time of the meditation. You can use a pendulum to help, if required. I normally find that one candle seems to choose me, and I am drawn to it and no other. Place it in the center of your altar and light it.

Sit quietly in front of your altar, and gaze at the candle, noticing its color, the brightness and color of the flame, and how it dances and flickers. Take several slow, deep breaths to help you relax. Each time you inhale you are absorbing color from the candle, and gaining all the qualities of that color. As you inhale, imagine all of this healing energy reaching every part of your body and aura. Visualize all of the negativity being eliminated from your body each time you exhale.

Allow yourself to relax and enjoy this healing energy as it restores and revitalizes every part of your body. Think of all the blessings in your life as you meditate and gaze at the candle. Give thanks for all of the good things that make life worthwhile. Express your gratitude for family, friends, and other loved ones. Give thanks for your hobbies, interests, and talents. Give thanks for all the love there is in the world.

When you feel ready, stand up, stretch, thank the candle as you snuff out the flame, and carry on with your day. You cannot perform this meditation too often.

Another method of performing this meditation is to choose a candle randomly. Place several different colored candles in a box, close your eyes as you mix them up, and then select one. The color you choose will be the color that your body needs at this time. Here are some keywords that you can think of as you inhale the essence of the candle:

Red: vitality, creativity, enthusiasm, energy

Orange: endurance, co-operation, diplomacy, self-esteem

Yellow: happiness, joy, confidence, self-expression

Green: health, self-love, self-worth, determination

Blue: serenity, wholeness, balance, inspiration

Indigo: love, support, relaxation, family

Violet: spirituality, intuition, insights, secrets

Pink: love, romance, harmony, pleasure, indulgence

Bronze (autumn colors): security, humanitarianism

Silver: intuition, dreams, inspiration

Gold: accomplishment, success, wealth, achievement

White: purity, protection, angel guardians, God

Black: change, new starts, release, freedom

Emotional Healing

Life is full of small annoyances and problems. Rather than dwelling on these problems, it is much healthier to use candle magic to eliminate them from your life.

To do this, you need to write a letter to the person who caused the problem, or who annoyed you. This person will not be reading the letter, so you can write down anything you wish. However, be fair. There is no need for exaggeration or bad language.

Here is an example. Suppose I was treated badly today at the bank. I was having a bad day anyway, and the last straw was when one of the tellers closed her window just as I reached it. It probably cost me only an extra couple of minutes in waiting time, but I was annoyed and thought about it for a while afterwards. Normally, I'd forget something like this in a matter of minutes, but because everything had been going wrong, I was hanging on to this imagined slight. To get rid of this self-inflicted needless aggravation, I can write the teller a letter:

> Dear Bank Teller,
>
> I was hurt and annoyed when you closed your window just as I reached it this afternoon. I had only a small deposit to make, and it would have taken you thirty seconds at the most to process. There was no one else waiting, and it wouldn't have hurt you to have attended to me. As a result of this bad service on your part, I have spent the afternoon thinking unpleasant thoughts about you and the bank. I think you should show

more consideration for your customers. After
all, we are the people who pay your salary. I
know you need time off for lunch and afternoon
tea, but my time is also worth something. I am
still extremely annoyed.

Yours sincerely.

The process of writing the letter allows you to express
your anger and hurt on paper, which gets it out of your
system. You can now release it to the universe, without
causing any harm to anyone.

You do this by lighting a white candle. Sit in front of it
and read the letter you have just written. Once you have
done this, fold it and put it into an envelope. Seal it, and
then burn it in the candle flame. As it burns, say: "I release my hurt and anger into the universe. I forgive
myself, and everyone else involved in this incident. This
matter is now over, and forgotten."

You will find this an exhilarating exercise. Instead of
bottling up your grievance and dwelling on it for hours,
days, or even years, you have released it, and let it go. This
is excess baggage that you no longer need carry, and the
rewards are more energy, contentment, and peace of mind.

You can heal all sorts of emotional problems in the
same way. Write a letter, explaining how you feel, and
then send it out to the universe while asking for forgiveness for everyone concerned. I have found this extremely
helpful for many small problems, but have never had to
do it for larger emotional issues. However, one of my students did. She was abused by her father when she was a

child, and had kept this as a guilty secret for her entire life. After performing this ritual a number of times, she finally made a breakthrough. We all wept when she told the class how this exercise had finally given her peace of mind.

Restoring the Soul Meditation

All you need is a white candle for this powerful, energizing meditation. Place the candle on your altar and light it. Sit down comfortably in front of your altar and spend a minute or two gazing at the candle.

When you feel ready, take three deep breaths, inhaling the purity and goodness of the white energy deep into your lungs. Hold each breath for a few moments and then exhale slowly.

You are now going to breathe in and absorb all the colors of the rainbow, one at a time. Start by closing your eyes and taking a deep breath. Imagine that you are inhaling perfect, undiluted red energy. Visualize this perfect red energy spreading to every part of your body. Exhale slowly. Breathe in red energy again, but this time imagine that you are breathing in universal love at the same time. Allow this universal love to merge with the red and again travel throughout your body. As you exhale, allow all your fears, doubts, and worries to leave your body.

Open your eyes, and gaze at the white candle for at least sixty seconds. When you feel ready, close your eyes again, and breathe in pure orange. Allow this to spread easily and effortlessly throughout your entire body. Exhale slowly. Take another deep breath, breathing in orange energy again, but this time inhaling joy, happiness and laughter with it. Allow this to spread throughout your body. As you exhale, allow all past disappointments, upsets and grievances to disappear. Open your eyes and gaze at the candle for at least sixty seconds, before repeating with yellow energy.

Each color represents positive qualities that you inhale into your body, and (with one exception) negative qualities that you exhale:

Red: inhale love
Exhale fear, doubt, and worry

Orange: inhale joy, warmth, happiness, and laughter
Exhale disappointments, upsets, and grievances

Yellow: inhale wholeness
Exhale disease and negativity

Green: inhale harmony, contentment, and emotional balance
Exhale disharmony and conflict

Blue: inhale peace
Exhale anger and conflict

Indigo: inhale impersonal, universal love
Exhale lust, sloth, and indifference

Violet: inhale spirituality, intuition, and enlightenment
Exhale love for humanity

As you exhale violet energy, imagine this divine love spreading to encompass the entire world.

Allow at least a minute between each color, and finish by inhaling pure white light. Visualize the light spreading throughout your body and then expanding out through your aura to encompass the entire world with love, peace and protection.

You should not wait until you need to restore your mind, body, and soul before doing this meditation. It can be done at any time, and as often as you wish. It will have a beneficial effect on every part of your life.

Healing Minor Ailments

Everyone has minor health problems from time to time. It might be a nagging cough that lingers on and on, a bout of influenza, a twisted ankle, or some other problem that will ultimately heal itself. You can speed up this process by performing candle magic on yourself.

You need three white candles, and a slightly taller candle to represent you. Inscribe some personal information about yourself on your candle, and include the words "perfect health."

Place the three white candles so that they form a small triangle in the center of your altar. The triangle should point toward the back of the altar. Place the candle that represents you in the middle of this triangle, and light it first, followed by the others.

Sit down comfortably and gaze at the candles. Visualize yourself surrounded by healing, protective energy, just as the candle that symbolizes you is surrounded by the protective white candles. Feel yourself surrounded by white light, just as if you are surrounded by enormous white candles, and allow the healing energy to drift into every part of your body. Say out loud: "I am surrounded at all times by divine healing energy. I know that I am whole, I am healed, I am perfect. I am fully restored to vibrant, glowing health. Thank you (whichever deity you wish) for restoring my health and vitality."

Remain seated in front of the candles for as long as you wish. Continue to visualize yourself in a state of perfect health. When you are ready, give thanks once more, and then snuff out the white candles, followed by the one that represents you.

Candle Ritual for Specific Areas

Different parts of the body are represented by different colors that are related to the chakras. You can make use of this to help heal specific ailments. All you need do is select a candle of the right color, place it on your altar, light it, and gaze at it for several minutes while sending thoughts of healing to the afflicted organs. Take several breaths, to consciously absorb the candle color. As you exhale, imagine the dis-ease leaving your body.

Keep the candle burning for as long as possible. Repeat every day until your health has been restored.

Red: legs, bones, teeth, gonads

Orange: pelvis, immune system, kidneys, spleen, sex organs

Yellow: solar plexus, stomach, liver, gall bladder, pancreas

Green: heart, lungs, circulation, thymus gland

Blue: throat, eyes, ears, thyroid

Indigo: eyes, brain, pituitary gland, head

Violet: brain, eyes, pineal gland

Healing Major Illness

Obviously, you should follow medical advice when dealing with any serious illness. Candle burning should be used as an adjunct to this. It would be irresponsible, and potentially dangerous, to rely entirely on candles to heal a major illness.

You need two candles to represent you. One, depicting you in perfect health, should be larger than the one that represents you as you are now. These should be inscribed to further identify them with you. The larger candle should also have the words "perfect health" inscribed on it. You will also need candles to represent loved ones in your life, and four white candles.

The white candles are placed in position close to the four corners of your altar. The candle representing you, as you are now, is placed in the center. The candles that represent the important people in your life are placed in a semi-circle behind this. The candle representing you in perfect health is placed to one side, off the altar, until it is required.

Light the candle that represents you, followed by the candles that symbolize the special people in your life. Finally, light the four white protective candles.

Sit down comfortably in front of your altar and gaze at the candles for a minute or two. When you feel ready, speak to the candle that represents you, telling it that you are not happy with your illness and that you want to be restored to perfect health. Pause, to see if a response comes into your mind. Speak to the candles that depict the important people in your life. Ask them to send healing energies to you. Again, wait for a response. Talk to the four white candles and thank them for their protection. Ask them to send healing energies to you, too.

Close your eyes for a few seconds and give thanks to God, however you visualize him or her to be. Thank whichever deity you prefer for all the blessings in your life, and for restoring you to perfect, vibrant health.

Pause for a few moments, and gaze at the candles. When you feel ready, snuff out the center candle that represents the sick you. Thank it for its help. Replace it with the other candle that represents you, fully restored to health. Light it, and then sit down again.

Talk to the new candle, thanking it for restoring you to perfect health. Although you are not yet healed, you must talk to this candle as if it has already happened, and that you are full of vitality again. Tell this candle your hopes and plans for the future, and thank it again for making it all possible.

When you are ready, thank the white candles again for their protection, the special people candles for their healing thoughts, and your candle for restoring you to health. Stand up and give thanks to whichever deity you wish.

Put out the candles, starting with the special people candles, followed by the white ones, and finally the candle that symbolizes you.

Repeat this ritual as often as possible until you are restored to good health again.

Healing with Archangel Raphael

In the hierarchy of angels, the best known are the archangels Michael, Gabriel, Raphael, and Uriel. Two of these, Michael and Gabriel, are mentioned by name in the Bible. The archangels are powerful beings of light who are willing to help you any time you ask for it. Each of them has a specific function to perform. Michael is responsible for protection, courage, truth and justice. Gabriel symbolizes strength, purification, prophecy and commitment, Uriel symbolizes love, beauty, service, and tranquility. Raphael is concerned with healing, wholeness, unity, and acceptance. Raphael's name means "healing power of God."

You can call on Raphael any time you feel unwell, out of touch with your soul or spirituality, or are emotionally drained.

You need to approach the archangels with respect. Consequently, clean and air the room you will be working in, and have a bath or shower before performing this ritual. You might like to play some gentle meditation music and burn some incense.

You need three candles: a violet one to indicate the spiritual nature of the ritual, one to indicate you, or the person who requires healing, and a green candle to symbolize Raphael. (Raphael's candle is green as this is the color of healing and also the color of the heart chakra.)

Before you start, write a letter to Raphael stating exactly what you desire. Thank him for his support and guidance, and ask for help in curing you (or whoever it is you wish to heal) of your illness. Write the letter as if you were writing to a close friend. The letter should not be formal or business-like. A warm, friendly approach is the best.

Place the three candles in a row on your altar. The candle representing you should be on your left, the violet candle in the middle, and the candle that symbolizes Raphael to your right. Light all three candles, and sit down in front of them. Take several deep breaths to help you relax. When you feel comfortable, ask Raphael for his aid. (I have referred to Raphael as "he" for convenience. However, angels are of no sex, so you may refer to Raphael as he or she.)

You will possibly experience a sign that Raphael is with you. The temperature of the room might change slightly, you might sense an invisible presence, or you might hear a voice in your mind. Pause for a minute or two, to ensure that Raphael is with you. Then read the letter you wrote out loud. When you have finished, ask

Raphael to help you. Speak simply, openly, and honestly. You can be as emotional as you wish. Tell Raphael everything that is on your mind.

When you have finished, thank Raphael for listening to you, and ask him to protect all the important people in your life. You can extend this, if you wish, and ask for protection for all humanity.

Sit quietly in front of your altar for several minutes. Pay attention to the thoughts that come into your mind. Gradually, you will sense that everything is going the way it should be, and that you are protected and loved by Raphael.

When you feel ready, get up, snuff out the candles from left to right, and carry on with your day. You will probably feel Raphael's presence as you go about your day. Odd thoughts may come into your mind, and you will possibly feel a beautiful, healing light around you.

Once you are restored to health, thank Raphael again. You may find that you have a natural healing ability and can call on Raphael to help you heal others. You will gain enormous satisfaction from doing this. Tell as many people as possible about Raphael and how they can bring him into their own life to provide wholeness and healing.

Restoring Vitality

It takes time to recover from any illness, and candle burning can help you restore your health and vitality. You will need three candles, one each of green, blue, and violet.

Place these on your altar and light them. Sit down comfortably in front of them, and give thanks to whichever deity you wish for restoring you to good health again.

Gaze at the green candle for several seconds, and then take a deep breath, visualizing your body filling up with green energy. Hold your breath for a short while, and then exhale slowly. Look at the blue candle for several seconds before taking another deep breath, this time absorbing blue energy. Hold the breath, and exhale slowly. Turn your attention to the violet candle, and then take a deep breath, allowing violet energy to reach every part of your body. Exhale slowly.

Spend a few minutes in front of the candles, thinking about what you will do once you are fully restored to perfect health, and have regained all the energy you lost while you were unwell. It is important that you keep thinking positive thoughts as you regain your strength and vitality.

When you feel ready, give thanks, and snuff out the candles.

Health Protection Ritual

This ritual uses white candles that are placed around you to create a circle of protection. The candles are burned while you sit or lie down in the center of the circle. The number of candles used is up to you. You can use a dozen or more, if you wish. However, I find that I usually use three to seven candles.

Three candles create a triangle, which is one of the most powerful geometric symbols. Traditionally, it has been considered a sign of God in both Christianity and Judaism.

Four candles create a square, which is an ancient sign to represent the earth. It indicates the four directions and is stabilizing, balancing, and grounding.

Five candles create a pentagram, or pentacle, which is a symbol of harmony. It originated in Mesopotamia some four thousand years ago. The Pythagoreans used the pentagram as a symbol of health and harmony.

Six candles create a hexagram, or the Star of David, which is formed by two interlocking triangles. It has also been called Solomon's Seal, and has been associated with exorcism.

Seven candles make use of the sacred and mystical aspects of the number seven. This number has always been considered important because of the seven celestial bodies that were visible to the ancients (Sun, Moon, Mars, Mercury, Jupiter, Venus, and Saturn). In the Bible, God created the world in seven days. Seven was a symbol of immortality in ancient Egypt, and was sacred to the god Osiris. Seven was also considered sacred to Mithras, Apollo, and Buddha. In the Hindu tradition, the sun had seven rays, and the world mountain seven faces. In Islam, seven is considered the number of perfection.

Choose the number of candles that seems right for you. Place them in a circle around where you will be sitting, and light them with intent. You are wanting the candles to help you become fully restored in mind, body, and spirit.

Once the candles have been lit, relax in the center and take three deep breaths, imagining yourself surrounded by a healing and protective white light. Inhale this white energy with each breath, and visualize all disharmony and dis-ease leaving your body on each exhalation.

Remain in the circle for ten to fifteen minutes, focusing on your desire for vibrant health. Do this at least once a day until your health is back to normal. It is a good idea to do this ritual for a few days afterward, also, to help you regain your strength and energy.

Healing Other People

This ritual has to be performed once a day for seven days. The best day to start is a Sunday. Light an orange or gold candle and place it on your altar. Sit down in front of the altar, gaze at the candle, and visualize the person you are seeking to help enjoying perfect health.

Take three deep breaths, and then recite the 23rd psalm. Alternatively, you can create a small poem about the sick person and recite that. The quality of the poem is not important. Your intent in writing and reciting the poem is more important than the words that you use.

Allow the candle to burn for as long as possible before snuffing it out.

Circle of Protection Ritual

This ritual can be done on its own, but is usually done to finish off a healing session. You need one white candle.

Ask the person being healed to lie on his or her stomach, with arms and legs slightly spread. Light the candle, and hold it several inches above the top of his or her head. Move the candle around the person's body, starting on the left side of his or her head, and down the neck to the shoulders, down the outside of the arm and hand, then up again to the armpit, and down the side of the body to the left foot. Bring the candle up between the legs to the groin, and then back down again to the right foot. Continue outlining the body in this way until you have returned to the top of the person's head.

Finish off by walking around the person, with the candle held high, to enshroud him or her inside a circle of protection.

Let the person rest for a minute or two before getting up.

Absent Healing Meditation

Ideally, this ritual involves four candles, and a photograph of the person to be healed. If you do not have a photograph, write down the person's full name on a sheet of paper, and add any personal details that you know about this person. The photograph, or sheet of paper, is referred to as the "witness."

One candle needs to be white, but the other three can be any colors that you desire. You might choose them using the person's birth details or numerology. Alternatively, you might choose them because of their healing qualities (green, for example). It does not matter what colors you choose, as long as you can relate them to the person requiring healing energies.

Arrange the four candles to form a diamond shape on your altar. The white candle should be at the back. Place the witness in the center, and light the candles, starting with the white one.

Sit in front of your altar, and think of the person you are sending healing energies to. Focus on the positive. Think of happy moments you have spent with this person, and the kind acts he or she has done.

Pick up the witness and look at it for several seconds, then blow out the candle nearest the front of the altar. Imagine that you are blowing healing energies to your friend. Blow out the left-hand candle next, followed by the right. Last of all, blow out the white candle. With each one, visualize yourself blowing healing energies into the universe so that they can heal your friend.

Solemnly give thanks, and then carry on with your day, confident that you have done something good for your friend. Repeat as often as possible until your friend has recovered.

Healing Pets and Other Animals

The pendulum is a useful tool when dealing with animals, who cannot tell you what is wrong with them. You can ask the pendulum if you should take your pet to the veterinarian, for instance. If your pet turns down a food that it formerly liked, you can ask your pendulum why your pet is not eating it. You can ask your pendulum about any food to see if your pet will like it, and gain nourishment from it. You can ask your pendulum if candle magic would help your pet, and assuming you receive a positive response, you can ask which candles should be used.

Your pet does not need to be in the room when you are performing a healing ritual. Use a photograph of your pet as a witness, and place this in the center of your altar. Choose a candle to represent you and another to represent your pet. Inscribe both of these. On your pet's candle include the words "vibrant health." You will also need a white candle.

Place the white candle in the center of your altar toward the back, behind the witness. The candle representing your pet should be on your left, with your candle on the right, and the witness in the middle.

Light all three candles. Think about your pet for a few minutes, remembering the happy times, and the love you share. Give thanks for the joy and happiness you have been able to give each other.

Gaze at the white candle and ask for pure white healing energy to surround you and your pet. Take three deep breaths, inhaling the pure white energy.

Look at the candle that represents you and pledge to do whatever you can to restore your pet to good health. Stare at the candle that represents your pet, and visualize it becoming full of healing energy. Once this candle is overflowing with healing energy, turn to the white candle and say a sincere thank you for all the healing energy.

Keep all three candles burning for as long as possible. When you are ready, snuff out your candle, followed by your pet's candle, and finally the white candle. Repeat this ritual once a day until your pet has been restored to health.

You are not restricted to pets with this ritual. You can provide healing for any animals or plants you wish. If you do not have a photograph to act as a witness, write down as much as you can about the animal on a sheet of paper, and use that. For instance, if you wanted to offer healing for a sick hedgehog, you might write down: "Sick hedgehog, lives in hedge beside my house." This identifies the particular animal you are performing healing for.

Nothing could be more important than healing. Once you master some of the techniques in this chapter you will be able to help all living things with your gift. Make good use of it.

In the next chapter we will learn how to divine the future with candle magic.

Thirteen
Candle Divination

Candles possess hypnotic powers, and provide an endless source of fascination. It is not surprising that people have been using them for divination purposes for thousands of years. The shapes, colors, and dancing motion of the flames, the soft sounds they make, and the varying patterns that candle wax creates can all be interpreted. This art is known as candle-gazing or fire scrying.

The ancient Greeks devised a system of this, using four candles.[1] Three created a triangular shape, and the fourth was placed in the center. All four candles were lit, but only the center one was interpreted. If the flame burned brightly, it was considered a sign of success. A dim flame indicated disappointment, a flickering flame showed wavering fortunes, and a flame that went out signified death.

This is similar to the little-known art of lychnomancy, which has discarded the center candle, but retained the triangle. In this version, the three flames are analysed together. Wavering flames indicate change, a spiral-like effect is a warning, and rising and falling flames indicate danger. If a candle goes out, it is a sign of a loss, but one flame shining more brightly than the others is a sign of good luck.

I love listening to the sounds that candles make. Often, it is almost indiscernible, and I have to strain to hear the endless chatter. To me, this means that everything is going according to plan, whether I am aware of it or not. The louder the candles talk, the more problems there are that need to be overcome.

The brightness of the candle can be interpreted, too. It is a good omen if a candle is easy to light, and then burns with a strong flame. When candles are hard to light, and then burn with a weak flame, it is a sign that the time is not right for the magic. If possible, perform the ritual at another time. Weak flames generally produce weak results. If you have to proceed with your magic, be aware of this, and remain as clearly focused on your intent as possible.

If you have two or more candles that represent people on your altar, see if they have equally strong flames. If one is stronger than the others, it is a sign that he or she is potentially more powerful or important than the rest.

Pay particular attention to this person, and think about his or her motivations, to see if they are likely to be used for good or ill.

A flame may also be weak because the person it represents is unwell or lacking in energy. Alternatively, this person may not be receptive to your magic.

The colors that the flames produce are important, also, and can be interpreted. A greenish flame, for instance, denotes healing energy.

Candles that burn cleanly, and leave little wax, are an excellent sign. It means that the ritual has gone well. A small puddle of wax left as residue should be examined. The shape of it can often give a clue as to the outcome. Many years ago, the wax from a money candle I burned created an approximation of a dollar sign. I considered this an extremely good omen.

Some candles produce a large amount of smoke. Assuming that the candle is a good quality one, large quantities of smoke are a sign that a great deal of work will be required initially, but that the ultimate result will prove worthwhile.

Sometimes candles go out for no apparent reason. A sudden breeze can do this if you are working outdoors. All you have to do in this case is to relight the candle and continue with the ritual. If there is no apparent reason for the candle to go out, abort the ritual, and conduct it again later. This is a sign of opposition, and it is a waste of time to relight the candle and continue. If possible, choose the perfect time for the ritual, and do it again then.

Fire Scrying

Scryers usually gaze into a crystal ball or black mirror to divine the future. Scrying appears to have originated in ancient Persia, though it quickly spread around the known world. St. Augustine, Pliny, St. Thomas Aquinas, and Paracelsus all mentioned it. Paracelsus wrote a complete book on the subject (*How to Conjure the Crystal So That All Things May Be Seen In It*). Nostradamus scryed with a large brass bowl full of water. John Dee's assistant, Edward Kelly, scryed with crystal balls and mirrors. The hypnotic powers of a candle flame lend themselves very well to scrying.

You will need a warm, quiet room to work in. Ensure that you will not be disturbed for at least half an hour. Allow your intuition to choose the right candle for you to use. Place this in the center of your altar, light it, and then sit down. Take a few deep breaths to symbolically discard the cares and stresses of everyday life. Relax your body and mind as much as possible, and then gaze at the flame. You will gradually enter a hypnotic, daydream-like state, and images, symbols, pictures, figures, and words will flow into your mind.

Try not to consciously evaluate anything that comes to you until afterwards. When you first start doing this, you will find it hard to remain in this dream-like state for more than a few minutes. However, the more you practice, the easier it will become, and you will be able to enter this state freely whenever you wish, and remain in it for as long as you desire.

It may have occurred to you that if you can scry with a candle flame, you could also do it with a fire. After all, everyone has had the experience of sitting by a warm fire, watching the flames, and gradually drifting into a trance state. Naturally, the fire has to be burning brightly for this form of divination to work. My grandmother was good at pyromancy, which is the technical name for this art. She would sit beside the fireplace in the middle of winter with a cup of hot chocolate in her hand. One moment she'd be talking to us, but a second later she'd be in a world of her own, totally lost in the pictures that she could see in the flames of the fire. Occasionally, she would toss salt on the fire to revive the flames, but usually she would wait until the flames were dancing and flickering merrily. Grandma used the fire to see her own future, and declared that it was impossible to read the future of anyone else this way. If we wanted to do it, we had to gaze at the flames ourselves. One night a piece of coal fell out of the fire as she was staring at it, and ended up on the hearth close to her. She was ecstatic, as this meant good luck for at least twelve months.

If you want to experiment with pyromancy, choose a time when you will not be disturbed. Sit comfortably by the fire and think of a question. Be as specific as possible. Do not ask questions that require a yes-or-no answer. Instead of asking if the family will spend Christmas with you this year, ask "what will Christmas be like this year?"

Continue to think of your question as you gaze into the flames. Be receptive to whatever comes to you. You might see shadowy figures dancing in the flames. You might hear a response in the crackling flames. A sudden thought might appear in your mind.

As with candle magic, always say thank you to whichever deity you wish before leaving. You might want to write your impressions down as soon as you finish, as, like dreams, they can disappear quickly. Also, something that may not make much sense at the time might be obvious when considered later.

Ceromancy

Ceromancy is the art of interpreting melted wax. It is similar to tea leaf reading, because the shapes that are formed by the wax can be interpreted.

Traditionally, wax is melted in a brass bowl and then carefully poured into another bowl that is full of water. The shapes that are created by this are fascinating and incredibly varied. With a small amount of imagination, a wonderful story can be woven about the images that are created.

If you wish to try this, heat the wax in a double boiler, as it is too dangerous to melt wax over an open flame. Carefully, pour a small amount of the molten wax into a large container of water. The wax will instantly solidify, and the shape that is created can be analyzed. Take it out of the water and look at it from different angles. Use your imagination, and see what it reminds you of. Repeat as many times as necessary until you have created a reading for yourself.

A simpler version involves a candle and a bowl of water. Think of a question as you light the candle. After the candle has been burning for a few minutes, tilt it slightly and allow some molten wax to fall into the bowl of water. The first drops will be attracted to the side of the bowl and create a border. These are not interpreted directly, but give clues as to the nature of the outcome. A clear, unbroken border ensures a positive answer to the question, while a wavy border indicates changes of plans. A broken border indicates a negative outcome. As more wax drips into the water, various shapes are formed, and these are interpreted. Some shapes will be obvious, while others need a degree of imagination to determine what they might represent. Some people are naturally good at reading symbols, such as those created from wax droppings, while others have to practice to develop the skill.

You can use candle divination to part the veil of the future, and then use a variety of candle rituals to help you get where you want to go. Rituals for six different purposes are covered in the next chapter.

Fourteen

Candle Rituals

As you have already discovered, you can create candle rituals for almost any purpose. The ones included here are rituals that I have found helpful. However, feel free to experiment and devise rituals of your own. Your intent is much more important than the ritual itself. Consequently, you do not need to worry that a ritual you create might not be perfect in every way. As long as your purpose is completely clear in your mind, any ritual you create will work well. Naturally, you should try to perform them at the most propitious times. However, if your need is urgent, any time will do.

In this chapter we will look at rituals for six different purposes:

- Gaining protection
- Achieving goals
- Relieving problems created from previous lifetimes
- Releasing karma
- Attracting spirit guides and angel guardians
- Achieving happiness, success, prosperity, and love

Rituals for Protection

We all need protection from time to time. There could be any number of reasons for this, such as an abusive partner, a difficult boss, a nagging relative or friend, and even psychic attack. The first ritual is one for general protection, and the second one is for protection against someone known to you.

Protect Yourself Ritual

Choose a candle to represent you. Ideally, this candle should be inscribed. Place it in the center of your altar, and surround it with eight white candles that are noticeably smaller than the candle that symbolizes you. Four white candles will do, if you do not have eight.

Light the candle that represents you, and then light the others in a clockwise direction, starting with the candle that is in the north position.

Sit down a few feet away from the candles and gaze at the candle in the center position that symbolizes you.

Notice how it is shielded and protected by the other candles. Continue to stare at the candles while imagining yourself surrounded by white light. Allow this light to surround you in the same way that the white candles surround the symbolic you.

When you sense the white light completely surrounding you, ask for divine protection. If you come from a Christian tradition, you might like to say the Lord's Prayer first. When you are ready, say the following words (or something similar): "I feel the need for divine protection at this time, and ask (whichever deity you choose) to strengthen, guide, and protect me for as long as is necessary." If you have a specific problem that you need protection from, discuss it with the deity. Pause every now and again to see what response comes into your mind.

When you feel ready, put out the white candles, one by one, again starting from the north and going around in a clockwise direction. As you snuff each candle out, whisper "thank you." Finally, pick up the candle that represents you. Hold it high, while offering a sincere thank you to your deity for providing you with the necessary protection. Put out the candle, and keep it in a safe place. As this candle represents you, you do not want anyone else to handle it.

Specific Protection Ritual

This ritual should be performed only when asking for protection from a specific person.

You need several candles for this ritual: seven candles of different colors to represent the rainbow and the chakras, a large white candle to symbolize you, and a small candle of whichever color you think fit to symbolize the person from whom you require protection. You might like to inscribe your name or date of birth on your candle to further identify it with yourself.

The rainbow candles are placed in a line across the back of your altar, with the red candle on your left when you are facing the altar, and the violet candle to your right. Place the candle that represents you in the center of the altar. The other candle is placed on its side, immediately in front of your candle.

Light the seven candles of the rainbow, starting with the red one. Pause after lighting it, and ask for protection for your root chakra. Visualize a ball of bright red in this part of your body. Repeat this with the other six candles of the rainbow. Once you have done this, light the candle that symbolizes you.

Sit down for a few minutes, gazing at the candles. Visualize yourself surrounded and enveloped by a clear white protective light. When you feel ready, pick up the candle that has been lying on its side. This is the candle that represents the person you require protection from. Notice how small and puny this candle looks compared to the others.

Light it in the flame of the red candle. Look at it for several seconds, then say: "The red in you has lost all its power." Blow the candle out, in the most contemptuous way you can. Light it again, using the flame of the orange candle. As before, look at it for several seconds, before "The orange in you has lost all its power." Blow the candle out, trying to be even more contemptuous this time. Repeat with all the colors of the rainbow.

Once you have done this, hold this candle in front of your face and speak to it. You can say whatever you wish. Finish by saying, "You have lost all your power over me. I am strong and divinely protected. You are weak and insignificant. Your negativity will never affect me again."

If you wish, you can break the candle in half at this point, and dispose of each half in a different place. However, if the person has affected you badly, you may want to keep the candle and repeat the ritual every day until it has been completely burned. Another alternative is to burn the remains of this candle under a full moon. Burning the appropriate candle under a full moon is a good way to end any problem or difficulty.

Rituals for Achieving Goals

You can perform these rituals at any time. Traditionally, the best time is when the Moon is waxing, as these are spells of increase. However, regular repetition of these rituals is more important than the time you choose to perform them in. Whenever possible, I do these rituals at favorable times, but I will not hesitate about doing them at unfavorable times if there is no alternative.

Work or Business Goal Ritual

Choose a candle to represent you and your specific goal. You might choose a green or gold candle if your goal was more money, for instance. Alternatively, you can choose any candle to symbolize you and inscribe on it a message that spells out your desire.

Choose candles to represent anyone else who is involved in the outcome. If you are asking for a pay increase, for instance, you would need a candle to represent your boss. If you wanted your business to be more successful, you might want candles to represent key staff members, customers, and possibly your family.

You also need two candles of the same color. However, they need to be as different in size as possible. These represent the current situation, and where you intend to be once the goal has been accomplished. If you want more money, you might inscribe a dollar sign on the sides of each candle. If you want a promotion that includes a bigger and better office, you might draw a small square to indicate your current office on the small candle, and a much larger square on the second candle.

Place the two candles of the same color on your altar. The smaller candle should be on your left, and the larger one on your right. Between these place the candle that represents you. Place the other candles around your symbolic candle. The most important people should be closest to your candle.

Light all the candles, and sit down in front of them. Extend your arms to symbolically encircle the group of candles, and start speaking to the candles. You can do this silently, if you wish. I prefer to speak, rather than say it in my mind. Hearing my own words seems to give added potency to the ritual. Let's assume you are asking for a pay increase. You might start by speaking to all the candles.

"I am asking you to help me obtain the pay raise I am entitled to. I believe that the work I do benefits the company, and that I deserve a substantial increase in pay." Speak in this manner for as long as you wish, and then direct your attention to the candle that represents your boss. "(Name of boss), I have been working for you for (length of time). I have done a good job, as I'm sure you realize. I believe I deserve a substantial pay raise of (specify the amount you desire). What do you think?"

Continue looking at this candle, and consider what thoughts come to your mind. When you are ready, look at the other candles that represent people involved, and ask them for their views. Again, see what thoughts occur to you.

Look at the candle that represents your boss, and thank him or her for the pay rise. Hold your arms out wide again to encircle the candles, and give thanks to the universe for all the blessings in your life.

Extinguish the small candle that represents your current financial situation, followed by the candles that represent the other people involved. Your boss should be the last one of these to be extinguished. This leaves two lit candles: the one that represents you, and the one that symbolizes the extra money you are about to receive. Pick up the candle that represents you with your left hand, and the other candle with your right. Hold them both as high as you can. With as much energy as possible, say, "Thank you! Thank you! Thank you!"

Place these candles back on the table, side by side. Stare at them for a minute or so, visualizing yourself as you will be in the near future, once you have your pay raise. When you feel ready, snuff out both candles, and carry on with your day.

Ritual for Other Goals

This ritual works well for anything that you desire greatly, and are prepared to work as hard and as long as necessary to achieve. Obviously, you must have a specific goal in mind. Choose a candle to represent this goal, and inscribe your ambition on it. Choose another candle to represent you. It should be about the same size as the first candle. Select a white candle to indicate your purity of heart. These candles are all that are required, although you can add additional candles to represent other people who are involved in the achievement if you wish. Naturally, you should have candles to represent other people if you are working on a group goal.

Place the white candle in the center of your altar, and light it. Gaze at it, while affirming the purity of your intentions. When you feel ready, light the candle that represents your goal and place this on the left side of the altar. Finally, light the candle that represents you, and place this to your right.

Sit in a position where you can see all three candles without moving your head. Say out loud (or to yourself, if preferred): "I deserve this goal. I am working hard to achieve it. This goal is now a reality."

Move the goal candle a few inches nearer the center of the altar. Repeat the words, and this time move the candle that represents you a few inches closer to the center.

Continue doing this until all three candles are in the center of your altar. Focus on the candle that represents you, and say: "I deserve this goal." Gaze at the white candle and say: "My intentions are good. This goal benefits all, and harms no one." Stare at the candle that represents your goal, and say: "This goal is mine. I can feel it, sense it, smell it, taste it, see it. This goal is mine!"

Sit in front of the candles and stare at them for as long as possible while thinking about your goal, and how it will become a reality. Put the candles out when you find your attention drifting.

Repeat this ritual as frequently as possible until the goal becomes a reality.

Rituals for Relieving Past Life Problems

We all bring into this lifetime a huge amount of baggage from previous incarnations. Doctors have noticed the way in which babies look around immediately after birth. Some seem scared and alarmed, while others look around as if asking "what's it going to be like this time?"

We bring into this incarnation useful skills and talents that we can develop further in this lifetime. We also bring negative characteristics that hinder us and hold us back. Fortunately, it is possible to eliminate these blockages with candle magic.

Obviously, you have to know what these blockages are. If you do not know, or are unsure, consult a qualified hypnotherapist and ask for a past life regression. You will find it a fascinating and enlightening experience. Alternatively, there are a number of techniques you can use to unlock the memories of your past lives. My book *Practical Guide to Past-Life Memories* contains twelve different methods.[1]

One of my clients suffered terribly from jealousy. We uncovered the reason for this in a previous lifetime she had in nineteenth-century Jamaica. Just recently, I was able to help a young man who had constant feelings of anger. Again, this was caused by something that happened in a previous incarnation. Once the source of the problem is known, you can use candle magic to control or eliminate the problem. Here is a ritual you can use.

Ritual for Past-life Problems

You need a candle to represent you. This should be inscribed with your full date of birth. In addition, inscribe your place of birth, and time of birth, if known. You will also need a smaller candle to represent you in the previous lifetime that you are dealing with. Inscribe on this candle any details that you know about the person you used to be. You might be fortunate and have your birth details. If so, these should be inscribed on the candle. You also need four white candles.

Place the two candles that represent you in the center of the altar. The previous life candle should be on your left as you face the altar. Around these place the white candles in the north, south, east, and west directions. Light the candles, starting with the one that represents your past life, followed by the one that represents you now. Finally, light the east, south, west, and north candles.

Sit in a position where you can see all the candles. Imagine yourself and your altar surrounded by pure white light. Focus on the candle that represents your previous life, and speak to it. "I am grateful for the lifetime you gave me," you might say. "It was a valuable learning experience for me. I know I did not learn all the lessons I was meant to, but I did my best. Unfortunately, some of the things I did not learn are still having a major effect on my life today. In particular, this time around, I am hampered and held back by (whatever the past-life problem may be). I want you to know that I am working on this, and ask you to release me from this burden, so that I can make further progress in this incarnation. Please set me free." Pause, and see what comes into your mind. You may receive a message, or perhaps feel a sense of comfort and ease.

When you feel ready, direct your attention to the candle that represents your current life. "Thank you for all the help and assistance you are giving me," you might say. "I am grateful to you for giving me opportunities to grow and develop. I am sure I will make many mistakes in this lifetime, but I want you to know that I am doing the very best I can. Now that I have been released from one of my major stumbling blocks, I am sure my progress will be more rapid in the future. Thank you for guiding and directing me."

Now look at the four white candles. "Thank you for your protection," you might say. "I value your help and support in everything I do."

Pause for about a minute, and then pick up the candle that relates to your previous incarnation. Blow the candle out, and whisper "thank you" to it. Place it to one side, outside the circle of white candles.

Contemplate the candle that represents you, surrounded by the white candles. When you feel ready, speak to the center candle. "I am glad that I am who I am. I am happy to be me. I am not perfect, but I'm striving to become better and better. With divine help and protection, I will achieve this. I have let go of the pain and trauma of the past, and am ready to move forward again in my life. Thank you for your help."

Snuff out the candles in the following order: north, west, south, east, and, finally, the candle that represents you. Repeat this ritual as often as necessary to eliminate the problem.

Rituals for Releasing Karma

Karma is the cause of law and effect. Everything balances out eventually, and it may take many lifetimes for this to occur. Consequently, something you do in one lifetime may not be repaid until the next lifetime. This can be extremely difficult, because you have no conscious memory of doing anything bad, yet are receiving more than your share of bad luck in the present lifetime.

Karma can not be magically released. They are lessons that need to be learned and the karma must be repaid. However, candle magic can help you come to terms with the present situation, and accept that the debt must be repaid before you can progress further.

Naturally, you must first become aware of the karmic debt. Numerology can help with some of these, as there are four karmic numbers: 13, 14, 16, and 19. If these occur behind the numbers of your Life Path, Expression, or Soul Urge, or you were born on one of these days in any month, you will have a karmic debt.

As 1 is the number of independence, a 19/1 shows that you thought only of yourself and abused power in a previous lifetime.

Four is the number of system and order. A 13/4 shows that you were frivolous and superficial in a previous lifetime, and did not apply yourself. Other people would have had to carry the burden.

Five is the number of freedom and variety. A 14/5 shows that you misused freedom in a past life, and probably overindulged in sensual pleasures at the expense of more important concerns.

Seven is the number of analysis and wisdom. A 16/7 shows that you misused sex, were self-centered, and caused suffering to others.

A past life regression can help you discover if there are any karmic debts from a previous lifetime that need to be repaid this time around. Naturally, you will be aware of any karmic debts that you created in this lifetime. The remedy for these is to make amends, as much as possible. Seek forgiveness from whoever it was you wronged, and also forgive yourself. Candle magic can help you with all of this.

Karmic Help Ritual

You will need a candle to represent you, three candles to symbolically represent the important people in your life, and four candles to symbolize divine help and protection. Choose the colors that seem right to you at the time you perform this ritual. Most people choose white candles to symbolize the divine, but you can pick any color you wish. Go with your feelings, rather than logic.

Place the candle that represents you in the center of your altar. Arrange the four divine help candles in the north, east, south, and west positions, and place the three other candles in a group to the left of the center candle.

Light all the candles, starting with the one that represents you, followed by the important people candles, and finally the divine help candles in east, south, west, and north order.

Sit comfortably, and gaze at the candle that symbolizes you. Acknowledge that you have made mistakes, both in this and other incarnations, and that you will strive to do better in the future. Naturally, you can do this only if you intend doing better.

Look at the candles that represent the important people in your life. Tell them how much you love and cherish them, and how important they are to you. As you do this, certain individuals may come into your mind. Say whatever needs to be said to them. There is no limit to the number of people you can speak to. The three candles symbolize a group of people, and this might be one or two, or maybe fifty people. Speak as freely as possible.

Finally, speak to the divine guidance candles. Admit your frailties and ask for divine help to enable you to repay your karmic debts. Ask for forgiveness, and give thanks for the help you will be receiving.

Sit in front of the candles for several minutes, allowing your thoughts to flow freely. You may receive some helpful insights that will help you overcome your difficulties. When you feel ready, snuff out the candles that represent the important people in your life. Thank them as you do this. Next put out the divine guidance candles, again giving thanks. Finally, hold the candle that symbolizes you high in the air for a few seconds. Give thanks that you are the person you are, and that you have the power and ability to make amends for any karmic debts. You are prepared to make the most of every opportunity life has to offer. Snuff out this candle and carry on with your day. Repeat this ritual as often as necessary.

Rituals to Attract Spirit Guides and Angel Guardians

Everyone feels lonely at times. When this occurs it is helpful to attract spirit guides and angel guardians to guide and comfort us. People often confuse these and think they are the same thing. Angel guardians are messengers between heaven and earth. They have never existed in human form. Spirit guides are people who have lived on this earth plane, but have passed over into the next life. You are surrounded by both all the time, but are unlikely to be aware of them until something goes wrong in your life. However, you do not need to wait until things go wrong. You can call on them at any time, and take advantage of their insight, guidance, wisdom, and protection. Some people would rather work with their spirit guides than their angel guardians, while other people are the opposite. Everyone is different. The underlying spiritual message is the same whether you work with spirit guides, angel guardians, nature spirits, or anything else that interests you. They are symbolic representations of the love, care, and guidance that the universe wants you to have. These rituals will help you contact your spirit guides and angel guardians and enable them to guide and advise you all the way through life.

Spirit Guide Attraction Ritual

In addition to a candle to represent you, you will need four white candles to represent divine energy, and a yellow candle to symbolize your spirit guides. A quartz crystal and incense are helpful, but not essential.

Place the candle that represents you in the center of your altar. Place the four white candles around it in the north, east, south, and west positions. Place the yellow candle on your left side, outside the circle created by the white candles. If you have a crystal, place that at the front of the altar. Light the incense, if you are using it. Incense is extremely helpful in contacting angelic energy, one of the reasons it is frequently used in churches.

Start by lighting the candle that represents you. Sit down and watch the flame as it dances on top of the candle. This candle symbolizes you. Visualize yourself in the center of your world. See all the people who you interact with on a daily basis, and imagine all of you surrounded by a pure white light of protection. Once you can clearly sense this, light the four white candles, starting in the east and moving around in a clockwise direction.

Pause, and look at the flames of the white candles. These candles symbolize the divine protection that surrounds you all the time, and is there whenever you need it. Finally, light the yellow candle, and look at the flame as it dances merrily, even though it is outside the circle of protection.

Your spirit guides are willing and able to help you in any way they can. All you have to do is ask. Pick up this yellow candle and hold it in both hands. Thank it for being there for you. When you feel ready, place it inside the circle of white candles, next to the candle that represents you. Watch these two candles for a minute or two. Imagine the essence of the yellow candle flowing effortlessly into the candle that represents you. Once you have done this, picture your spirit guides magically entering every cell of your body, ready to help you in every way possible. With the help of your spirit guides you can achieve much more than you ever thought possible. Thank your spirit guides again for being there for you. If you are using a crystal, hold it briefly over the smoke of each candle, to imbue it with their energy. Then place it back in position.

The ritual is now over, and you can put out the candles (starting with the white candles, followed by the yellow, and finally the candle that represents you). This ritual can be done in just a few minutes. However, make sure that you do not rush it. Allow as much time as necessary. Pause now and then, and remain receptive to any ideas or insights that occur to you. This ritual is similar to a meditation, and at the end of it you will feel revitalized and uplifted.

Angel Guardian Ritual

If your goals include spiritual growth, you will want to perform this ritual regularly. You will need a candle to represent you, six white candles, incense, and a small object that you can carry around with you, once the ritual is over. I have a small piece of jade that someone gave to me at an airport many years ago. A small crystal is ideal, but anything that will fit in your pocket, purse, or handbag will do. It may not be worth anything, but should be considered precious to you.

Place the candle that represents you in the center of the altar. It should be inscribed to identify it with you. Place the six white candles in a row along the front of the altar. Place the precious object between them and the candle that symbolizes you.

Start by burning some incense. Wait about five minutes before lighting the candles. Light your candle first, followed by the white candles, starting from the left-hand side of the row.

When all the candles are lit, sit down comfortably and look at them. If you are from a Christian tradition, you might want to start by reciting the 23rd Psalm. If you come from a different tradition, you might want to start with reverent words that are familiar and comforting to you. Alternatively, you might simply say, "Hello, architect of the universe," and carry on from there. Think about your need for angelic guidance or protection, and ask for divine aid to be with you always. I find it helpful to express these thoughts out loud. This is not necessary, but I feel that it adds extra potency to the ritual. Ask for your angel guardians to make themselves known to you, and thank them for their assistance and support.

Pick up the precious object and hold it over the smoke of each candle, saying "thank you" over each one. Save the candle that represents you until last. Hold the object up high with both hands, and give thanks once again. The object is now imbued with spiritual energy. From now on, you will probably be able to sense this whenever you hold it.

Snuff out the candles, starting with the white ones. Put out the candle on the right-hand side first and go along the line. Once they are all out, snuff out the candle that symbolizes you. Place the precious object in your purse, handbag, wallet, or pocket, and carry on with your day.

If you do this ritual on a regular basis, you will feel your angel guardians around you as soon as you start getting ready to perform it.

Rituals for Happiness, Success, Prosperity, and Love

We should all be leading lives full of love, success, happiness, and abundance. Unfortunately, many people miss out on these blessings. These rituals are designed to attract these beneficial qualities into your life. Repeat them on a regular basis until you achieve your goals.

Ritual for Happiness

You will need a candle to represent you. No matter how you may be feeling, choose a cheerful, happy color to symbolize you. Inscribe it with some of your personal details to align it even more closely with you. As you are doing this, think about what would make you happy. You might want to attract some friends. Conversely, you might be constantly surrounded by people, and want peace and quiet. Think about the things that would make you happy, and choose candles to symbolize them. If you are not sure what would make you happy, choose several colorful candles to represent whatever it is that would make you happy. Remember that material things will not make you happy for long. There is a saying that goes: "The most important things in life are not things." Think carefully before deciding what would make you happy.

Place the candle that represents you in the center of your altar. Place the other candles in a semi-circle behind it. Light the candle that represents you, followed by the others. Sit down and gaze at the candles. Observe the flickering flames, and notice how each candle flame seems to dance in a slightly different way to the others.

If you come from a Christian tradition, you might want to start by reciting psalm 144. The final verse of this psalm is: "Happy is that people, that is in such a case: yea, happy is that people, whose God is the Lord." You might like to start by pondering the advice of one of my heroes, Marcus Aurelius. He suggested that whenever you want to cheer yourself up you should think of the good qualities of your friends and other people in your life.[2] Alternatively, you might want to think about moments of happiness you've experienced in the past. For most people these are not earth-shattering events. It might be listening to a certain piece of music, enjoying a meal with a few friends, or a chance meeting with someone you haven't seen for a long time.

When you feel ready, tell yourself that you are a good person who deserves happiness. Spread your arms out wide, and say: "From today onward, I am going to attract good things to me. Every aspect of my life is going to get better and better. I deserve happiness. I am a good person, and I deserve the best that life can offer. I am a happy person. I choose to be happy, no matter what occurs in my life. I am happy."

Place your hands in your lap and close your eyes for a few moments. Sense what is going on in your body. If you detect feelings of well being, you can finish the ritual. If your body appears to be denying the words you have just spoken, repeat them again, and test your body afterward. Keep on doing this until your body tells you that the ritual is over.

Put out the candles, leaving the one that represents you until last, and continue with your day. Repeat this ritual as often as possible, until you feel happy and contented most of the time.

Ritual for Success

It is natural to desire success. No matter how successful you may be now, you will probably want to become even more successful. Life has its shares of ups and downs, and nothing is permanent. You might be a dismal failure today, but that doesn't mean that you can't become hugely successful tomorrow. No matter where you are at the moment, this ritual will help you progress further and become more successful in the future.

You will need a large candle to represent yourself. Choose a powerful color, such as gold or red, and inscribe the candle with details about you and your desire for success. If this is financial success, you might want to inscribe a dollar sign. If you want success in all areas of your life, you might choose an upward-pointing arrow to indicate where you want to go. This candle is placed in the center of your altar.

You will also need four white candles to symbolize divine protection. They are placed in the north, south, east, and west positions around your candle.

You also need an ornament of some sort that indicates success to you. I have a small onyx pyramid that I use for this. The pyramid points toward the sky, and I interpret this to indicate upward progress. You need an ornament that can be displayed openly in your office or home without attracting undue attention from others. Every time you see it, you will automatically be reminded of your desire for success. The ornament should be placed at the front of your altar in the center.

You also need candles of the right colors to represent your Life Path, Expression, Soul Urge, and Day of Birth. These are placed in the four corners of your altar.

Incense is optional. I like to use it for this particular ritual, as I want to gain help from every source possible.

Start the ritual by lighting the four corner candles and the one in the center (that represents you). After this, light the four white candles, in north, east, south, and west order.

Spend a few moments thinking about success and what it means to you. Your idea of success is likely to be different to mine. Allow yourself to fantasize a little, as you gaze at the candles, and think how your life will change once you achieve the success you desire.

Hold your arms out wide to symbolically encircle your altar, and ask for divine help to achieve your goals. Be as specific as possible. If you desire money, specify the amount. If you want a new home, talk about the type of house you want, and everything you want inside it.

Now you have to state what you are prepared to do in order to reach this level of success. There is almost always a price to be paid, and if you desire extraordinary success you must be willing to pay the price.

Once you have done this, give thanks for the blessings that you are going to receive. Pick up the ornament and pass it through the smoke of each candle. Hold the ornament in both hands and solemnly say thank you again. Put out the candles in reverse order to the way you lit them, display the ornament where you will see it frequently, and carry on with your day. Repeat this ritual once a week until you have achieved the degree of success you desire.

Ritual for Prosperity

This ritual is similar to the success one. However, instead of using an ornament, you need three coins. I have three Chinese coins that I use purely for this ritual, but any coins will do. However, it is a good idea to use unusual coins as you need to keep them with you. If you use nickels or quarters you might accidentally spend them.

Arrange the candles in the same layout as the previous ritual, and light them. Sit in front of the candles and think about your desire for prosperity. Be specific about the exact amount of money you desire. Asking for a lot of money is not helpful, as the definition of "a lot" varies from person to person. Asking for a million dollars is specific. Do not be modest in your request. The universe will help you attain any amount you ask for. Think about what you will do once you achieve this financial goal. Consider the changes that this amount of money will make in your life. Think about the work that will be required to earn this amount of money.

Extend your arms and give thanks for all the blessings in your life. Start talking about your dreams of financial independence, and how you intend achieving it. Ask for divine protection and aid. Pick up the three coins and jingle them in your cupped hands. Pass them over the smoke from each candle, and give thanks once again.

Toss the coins in the air three times and catch them. Jingle them in your hands for a few moments, while imagining large amounts of money coming into your possession.

When you feel ready, put out the candles and carry on with your day. Keep the coins with you at all times.

Treasure Trove Ritual

This is a fascinating ritual that provides incredible results.

It has worked for me, and everyone I have shown it to, who has tried it, has experienced similar results.

First of all, sit down somewhere comfortable and write down a list of all the things you would like to have in life. More money? Write down the exact amount you would like. A soul mate? Write down all the qualities you would like your soul mate to have. A new house? New car? An overseas trip? It makes no difference what it is, just as long as you greatly desire it. It pays to create this list over a few days, as various ideas will come into your mind once you start thinking about it.

Once you have made your list, start looking for pictures in newspapers and magazines to illustrate what you are seeking. For instance, if you greatly desire a new home, find a picture of the sort of home you would like. When you have pictures of all the things you desire, stick them to a large sheet of cardboard. This is your treasure trove map. Arrange the pictures as aesthetically as possible, and feel free to add any decorations you wish. You might also choose to add monetary amounts to the pictures to indicate the approximate cost of each item. If you are fortunate, you might be able to display your completed treasure trove map in your home so that you see the objects you desire every time you glance in their direction. Most people prefer to keep their desires a secret, and do not want them on display for everyone to see. That is fine, too. In this case you need to roll up the treasure trove map, after performing the ritual, and put it away safely until the next time.

As well as the pictures of everything you desire, you need at least seven candles: one inscribed candle to represent you, a gold one to symbolize abundance, a red one to symbolize energy and power, and four white candles for protection. You can add as many candles to this as you wish. If one of your desires is a partner, for instance, you would probably want to burn a pink candle.

Place the treasure trove map on your altar. If it is too large, you might want to perform the whole ritual on the floor, rather than a table. Place a white candle in the center of each side to represent the four directions. Place the candle that symbolizes you in the center. The gold candle is placed on the far left corner, and the red one is placed in the far right corner. Any other candles can be placed on the front two corners, followed by a line across the back of the altar.

Light the four white candles first, followed by the one that symbolizes you. Follow this with the gold candle and the red one, as well as any other candles you have added.

Kneel in front of your altar (or in front of the treasure trove map if doing this on the floor). Give thanks to whichever deity you choose, and then sit down in a position where you can see your treasure trove map, as well as all the candles.

Look at the different pictures, and visualize yourself already in possession of each item. Allow yourself to fantasize about how your life will be once you have attained everything on your map.

When you feel ready, extend your arms to indicate the entire map, and say "thank you" out loud. This should be said sincerely, and with conviction, as if you had already received everything on the map.

Keep the candles burning for as long as possible. You may move around the room, but do not leave it while the candles are still burning.

When you feel ready to end the ritual, give thanks again for all the blessings in your life, and for the blessings that are yet to come. Put out the candles in the reverse order to the one you used when lighting them. Put the candles away carefully, so that you may use them again next time.

Repeat this ritual as often as possible until the items start to manifest. When this happens, you might change the pictures on your treasure trove map. You can do this at any time, adding new items and removing items that have already come to you.

Ritual for Love

Most people seek the love, support, loyalty and friendship that the right relationship provides. If you are still looking for that special someone, this ritual will help you find the right partner.

Choose a candle to represent you, and inscribe on it some personal details, as well as something to indicate what you are seeking. A love heart will satisfy this requirement, although anything that signifies love and romance will do.

You will also need eight pink candles. These candles are arranged in a circle around the candle that represents you. As well, you need a candle to symbolize your future partner. It is generally safer to choose a white candle for this person. A blue candle, for instance, might attract to you someone with a five life path, which may not be what you want. Inscribe something to indicate love and romance on this candle. You may also want to add any requirements that you consider essential to the relationship. You might specify an age range, for instance.

You may choose to use incense, and to display objects in the room that symbolize love and romance. Pairs of anything can be used to symbolize couples. Do not use anything that is connected with a previous relationship, as you do not want to attract anything negative from the past. A smiling or laughing photograph of you can be helpful. Place this on the left-hand side of your altar. A helpful touch is to cut a heart from paper or cardboard and write on it exactly what sort of person you are seeking. This should be placed underneath the candle that represents you.

This ritual should be performed in a light-hearted, carefree state of mind. You are getting ready to attract a special person into your life, so you should be cheerful and positive.

At the start of the ritual, the candle that symbolizes your future partner is placed outside the circle. Light the pink candles first, and then light the candle that represents you. Gaze at the candles and think about the qualities your ideal partner would possess. You might, for example, want someone who is between 35 and 50, financially independent, has a good physique, is a good conversationalist, and highly romantic. Think of all the qualities you desire in this person. It is important to be reasonably specific. If you are twenty-three years old, you might not want to attract an eighty-five-year-old partner.

Pick up the candle that symbolizes your future partner and light it. Hold it between both hands, and talk to it. "You represent my future partner," you might say. "I am looking for someone special. You symbolize that special someone who will love and cherish me. You must be kind, gentle, loving, and romantic. You will also need to be a good provider, have an excellent sense of humor, and be a gentle, but skillful lover. Age is not important, but I ideally want someone between twenty-five and forty years old. In return, I can offer this special person" (continue with what you are prepared to offer the right person).

After saying these words, pause for a few minutes, while continuing to gaze at the candles. Allow your thoughts to flow freely, and become aware of any insights or ideas that occur to you.

Place the candle you are holding in the center of the circle beside the one that symbolizes you. Visualize these two candles merging into one.

Close your eyes for a few moments and see if a picture of your future partner will come to you. People experience things in different ways, so you may see this person clearly in your mind. Alternatively, you might feel him or her around you, or just sense that this special person is close.

When you feel ready, open your eyes again. Give thanks to the universe for attracting to you what you desire. Do this sincerely, and as if your loved one was already with you.

Once you have done this, put out the pink candles. This leaves the candles that symbolize you and your future partner. Make a circle of your arms around them, and say "welcome!" Finally, snuff them out, and put them away carefully, ready to be used again.

This ritual should be repeated at least once a week until you find the right person. You can test people you meet by holding a pendulum over the future partner candle, and asking if he or she is the person you are waiting for. It is important that you do this only with people who you suspect are the correct person, as the pendulum will get annoyed if you use it frivolously.

All of these rituals can be made even more effective when you use candles you have made yourself. Many magicians enjoy making their own candles, but I have met at least as many who have never attempted to make their own. If you think you would enjoy making your own candles, the next chapter tells you how to do it.

Fifteen

How to Make Your Own Candles

Most of the time I buy my candles. However, on many occasions I have made my own candles. Sometimes this is solely for the pleasure I gain out of making something useful, but more frequently it is because I want to imbue the candles with special intent and energy. Fortunately, candles are not hard to make, as long as basic safety precautions are taken.

Most reasonable-sized towns have a store that specializes in selling candle-making supplies. Some of these offer classes in candle-making, and it is worth taking these to learn the finer points of the craft.

Naturally, you need to make the candles with your intent clearly in mind.

Beeswax Candles

I used to keep bees and consequently always had a supply of honeycomb sheets. Nowadays, you can buy these in a range of colors. Many apiaries sell beeswax sheets at reasonable prices. Beeswax candles are easy to make, although there is a knack to creating attractive-looking candles every time.

You will need three honeycomb sheets to make one candle. Place a honeycomb sheet on a flat surface and lay a wick along one of the shorter edges. Fold the edge of the honeycomb over the wick and press down tightly to hold it in place. Roll the honeycomb sheet tightly. Shortly before you have rolled to the end, overlap another honeycomb sheet, and keep doing this until the candle has reached the desired diameter. Usually, three sheets is sufficient.

Your supplier should also be able to supply beeswax in block and bead form. This can be used in conjunction with paraffin wax to make beautiful molded candles. These candles do not shrink as much as molded candles made solely from paraffin wax. The usual ratio is one part beeswax to four parts paraffin wax.

Molding Candles

Requirements

1. A double boiler. It is best to buy a double boiler especially for candle making. A slow-cooker appliance also works well. Never melt wax in a pot over an open flame.

2. Thermometer. Your supplier will be able to suggest the best type for your needs. Mine is intended for determining the heat of roasting meat, and consists of a metal rod with a circular dial on top.

3. Molds. You will be amazed at the range of molds available. They are made in metal, plastic, and rubber. You can also use a variety of containers of your choice, as long as they don't melt, and allow you to release the candle once it is made. Start with a simple mold. Once you gain experience, you can try more complicated molds, if you wish.

4. Mold release spray. This is a silicone spray, and should be readily available at your candle supplier.

5. Wick cutter. Sharp scissors work well for this.

6. Fire extinguisher. Hopefully, you will never need this. Baking soda is also good for smothering flames if you do have a fire.

7. Wax. The best wax to start with is paraffin wax. This is available from grocery, hardware, and craft stores. A specialist candle supplier will be able to tell you the advantages and disadvantages of various waxes. Most suppliers will sell mold wax that melts at around 140 degrees (60 C). This will make a good, solid candle that will release easily from any mold. There is a type of paraffin wax called "one-pour" which does not

shrink when it cools. Although it is more expensive, it does eliminate a number of potential problems. Dipping wax is used for making taper candles. It melts at 145 degrees (65 C) and because it sticks to itself is ideal for making dipped candles.

8. Wax additives. The range of these has increased dramatically in recent years. The most commonly used additive is stearine, sometimes called stearic acid. This hardens the wax and makes release from the mold easier. Your supplier will be able to advise you on the amount to use. Vybar is a useful additive that should be used if you desire beautiful white candles. Pourette's crystals can be added to the wax to help reduce shrinkage. They are melted separately to the wax, and then mixed in before pouring the candles. Naturally, you can also add other items to the wax, depending on the rituals you will be performing. Leaves, herbs, and coins are all examples of objects that can be added.

9. Wicks. Again, there are many types of wicks available. The most commonly used wicks for molded candles are flat braided and square braided. The square braided wicks are the most popular for molded candles. Flat braided wicks are better for rolled candles. The wick needs to be in proportion to the diameter of the candle. Use a small wick when using a narrow mold, and a larger wick when making larger candles.

You will need to experiment to determine the correct wick for each size candle.

10. Dyes. Dyeing is the most commonly used method of coloring candles, and it is best to use dyes made specifically for candle-making. Do not use crayons as dyes, as these can cause problems with the wick. You do not want your candles mysteriously going out in the middle of a ritual. Dyes are available in liquid, powder, cake, and chip form.

11. Scent. I prefer not to scent my candles, as I prefer using incense in my rituals. However, if you do want to scent your candles use liquid scent in preference to block scent. It is more expensive, but easier to use, and produces a more attractive scent. You can also scent your candles with various herbs and spices.

12. Paper towels. Candle making can be messy, and paper towels can be used in a variety of ways. You can use them to cover your working surface, to mop up spills, to wipe your hands, and to help you pick up items that may be hot.

Instructions

If your wax has come in the form of a large block, put it in a plastic bag and break up the wax with a mallet. Alternatively, slice pieces off with a knife. Put your wax into your double boiler, and add sufficient stearine. Usually, two to three tablespoons of stearine per pound of wax is sufficient. Heat until melted.

While your wax is heating, prepare the molds. Spray a small amount of silicone spray into your molds, then wick them. Follow the instructions for your molds to do this. The easiest way to wick nonstandard molds is to make a small hole in the bottom, and thread the wick through that. Seal the outside of the hole with rubber cement. Attach the other end to the center of a rod resting across the top of the mold. You may prefer to glue the wick to the base of the mold. Another alternative is to dip the wick in melted wax for a moment. Holt it taut until the wax dries. This creates a stiff wick that can be placed in the center of the mold, with the top end attached to a rod, as before. Square-braided wicks are the best for molded candles. If you are using a flat-braided wick, make sure that you have the nap of the braid pointing down. This is easy to do as the pattern looks like a series of downward-pointing arrows.

Prepare a water bath, filling the container to about half an inch of the top of the molds. Ensure that no water gets inside the mold while doing this.

Keep an eye on the heating wax, stirring it from time to time with a wooden spoon. Check the temperature frequently with your thermometer to ensure that you do not get anywhere near flashpoint. Flashpoint is the temperature at which wax will combust. This is 375 degrees for most paraffin wax. Make sure that you keep your wax well below this temperature—140 degrees is hot enough for most purposes.

Once your wax has reached pouring temperature, turn off the heat and add dye, if you are making colored candles. Stir well until all the dye has been dissolved. If you are using scent, add this immediately before pouring the candle.

Carefully, pour the wax into the mold. Do this slowly and steadily. If you can tilt the mold slightly while pouring the wax, you can avoid most of the tiny air bubbles that usually form. Fill the molds to about an inch from the top. When you have finished pouring the wax, tap the sides of the mold to release any air bubbles that might be caught inside. Wait sixty seconds to allow them to escape, and then place the mold in the water bath. The water bath gives the candles a smooth, shiny, even texture. Ensure that no water comes in contact with the wax, however, as this will ruin the candle. You will probably have to attach a weight to your molds to prevent them from tipping in the bath.

Leave the candles in the water bath for about two hours, and allow the rest of the cooling to take place at room temperature. Large candles can take up to eight hours to cool down sufficiently before removing them from the molds. I usually leave them overnight to ensure that they have completely hardened.

Allow the candle to completely solidify before removing it from the mold. The candle should slide out easily. If you have difficulty extracting the candle, place the mold in a refrigerator for half an hour and try again. (If the mold is a metal one, leave it in the refrigerator only until the mold feels cold. If you leave them in the cold too long, the candle will develop cracks.) A last resort is to heat the mold with hot water until the candle slides out.

It pays to keep a small amount of wax from the batch in reserve, because wax can shrink around the wick as it solidifies. As your candle cools, check every now and again to see if this is occurring. If necessary, pour some wax in to refill the gaps. You may have to do this a number of times. This problem does not arise with "one-pour" wax.

You may need to flatten the base of your candles. Heat a baking pan over boiling water. Hold the candle by the wick and allow the base to gently touch the pan until the base of the candle is smooth and flat. An alternative method is to use an old frying pan.

Any small marks or fingerprints on the candle can be removed with a soft cloth. Candle sheen can be obtained from your supplier to give your candles a shiny, protective coating, if you wish.

Dipping Candles

Dipping candles is an excellent way to make taper candles. You will need a container of melted wax. This container should be deep enough to hold about an inch more wax than the length of your candle. You will need to dip a wick in the melted wax a number of times to gradually create the candle.

There are two ways of starting. One is to attach a small weight to the end of the wick to ensure that it sinks down to the bottom of the container of molten wax. Alternatively, you can dip the wick into the wax, pull it out, and hold it taut until the wax dries and the wick becomes stiff. You can then dip it as many times as necessary.

Although dipping may seem like an easy way to make a candle, there is quite a bit to it. If you hold the wick in the wax for too long, it will cause the hardened wax from previous dips to melt. If you hold the wick in the wax for too short a time, you are likely to make unsightly candles.

The first time you dip the wick, leave it in the wax for three minutes. Bring it out and wait for it to cool. Once you can handle it, smooth the wax with your fingers, or by rolling it on a smooth surface.

Dip the candle again for about three seconds. Bring it out for three minutes. The next time you dip it, submerge only a third of the wick. Bring it out for three minutes. Dip again for three seconds, this time submerging two-thirds of the candle. Bring it out for three minutes. Dip the entire candle for three seconds.

Keep on working in this fashion. Dip one third of the candle for three seconds, followed by two-thirds, followed by the entire candle, allowing a gap of three minutes between each dip. Keep on doing this until the candle is the size you want it to be.

This may sound like a time-consuming, arduous business. Fortunately, you can dip two or more candles at the same time. Suspend as many wicks as are necessary from a rod, and dip them together. This speeds up the entire process. However, you can produce candles for only one purpose at a time. It is impossible to focus your intent on a number of different areas while you are making them.

Candle making is a fascinating pursuit, and I know a number of people who have become addicted to it. Keep notes of your successes and failures. Even the temperature of the room can affect the final result. Experiment with different combinations and mixtures, until you achieve the results you are looking for.

Conclusion

Now it's up to you. You now know everything you need to know about the gentle art of candle magic. Candle magic has been an important part of my life for forty years now, and it has helped me and many other people. I taught psychic development classes for years, and witnessed many of the successes my students had with candle magic. I saw financial problems brought under control. I witnessed amazing healings. One of my students who had been unemployed for years found work. Others found their life partner. These results all came about as a result of candle magic. Because I am aware of what candle magic has done for me, and have seen incredible results in so many other people, I know that it will also work for you.

Among other things, candle magic will help you:

- Find the right partner
- Improve an existing relationship
- Achieve inner peace and contentment
- Enjoy better relationships with others
- Give thanks for the blessings in your life
- Find the right job
- Achieve prosperity
- Protect yourself and others
- Become more (or less) fertile
- Connect with the divine
- Strengthen your spirituality
- Develop psychically
- Improve your health
- Eliminate bad habits
- Obtain what you desire
- Eliminate someone from your life
- Eliminate negative energy
- Gain positive energy
- Increase your luck
- Change your future

However, nothing will happen unless you start using candle magic for yourself. Think of something you desire or wish to achieve, and then perform a candle ritual. Start with small requests, and measure the results. It is a good idea to keep a grimoire to record your experiments in. A school exercise book will do, but you will feel better if you spend a few dollars more and buy an attractive book to write your findings in. Over a period of time this book will develop into a fascinating record of your magical growth and development.

Once you gain confidence and experience at candle burning, feel free to experiment. In these pages I've explained my thoughts on candle magic, but you will have ideas of your own. Everything you need to know to devise your own system of candle magic is here, in these pages. Use your creativity and intuition to devise rituals that are uniquely yours. You will gain enormous pleasure out of constructing them, and will find them far more powerful than any "off the shelf" rituals could ever be.

Candle magic is deceptively simple. Because of this, people think it is easy. However, like anything worthwhile, it takes time and effort to achieve good results.

Look after your candles. Ensure that you dress them before use. Put them away carefully after your rituals. Treat them with respect. Perform only good magic.

Magic is a powerful tool for change, and has the potential to enhance every area of your life. You will become aware of this as soon as you resolve to lead a magical life. If you follow the advice and suggestions in this book I know that candle magic will play an important part in your growth and development.

Elements and Signs for the Years 1900–2008

Element	Sign	Time Period
Metal	Rat	31 January 1900 to 18 February 1901
Metal	Ox	19 February 1901 to 7 February 1902
Water	Tiger	8 February 1902 to 28 January 1903
Water	Rabbit	29 January 1903 to 15 February 1904
Wood	Dragon	16 February 1904 to 3 February 1905
Wood	Snake	4 February 1905 to 24 January 1906
Fire	Horse	25 January 1906 to 12 February 1907
Fire	Sheep	13 February 1907 to 1 February 1908
Earth	Monkey	2 February 1908 to 21 January 1909
Earth	Rooster	22 January 1909 to 9 February 1910
Metal	Dog	10 February 1910 to 29 January 1911
Metal	Boar	30 January 1911 to 17 February 1912
Water	Rat	18 February 1912 to 5 February 1913
Water	Ox	6 February 1913 to 25 January 1914
Wood	Tiger	26 January 1914 to 13 February 1915
Wood	Rabbit	14 February 1915 to 2 February 1916
Fire	Dragon	3 February 1916 to 22 January 1917
Fire	Snake	23 January 1917 to 10 February 1918
Earth	Horse	11 February 1918 to 31 January 1919

Element	Sign	Time Period
Earth	Sheep	1 February 1919 to 19 February 1920
Metal	Monkey	20 February 1920 to 7 February 1921
Metal	Rooster	8 February 1921 to 27 January 1922
Water	Dog	28 January 1922 to 15 February 1923
Water	Boar	16 February 1923 to 4 February 1924
Wood	Rat	5 February 1924 to 24 January 1925
Wood	Ox	25 January 1925 to 12 February 1926
Fire	Tiger	13 February 1926 to 1 February 1927
Fire	Rabbit	2 February 1927 to 22 January 1928
Earth	Dragon	23 January 1928 to 9 February 1929
Earth	Snake	10 February 1929 to 29 January 1930
Metal	Horse	30 January 1930 to 16 February 1931
Metal	Sheep	17 February 1931 to 5 February 1932
Water	Monkey	6 February 1932 to 25 January 1933
Water	Rooster	26 January 1933 to 13 February 1934
Wood	Dog	14 February 1934 to 3 February 1935
Wood	Boar	4 February 1935 to 23 January 1936
Fire	Rat	24 January 1936 to 10 February 1937
Fire	Ox	11 February 1937 to 30 January 1938
Earth	Tiger	31 January 1938 to 18 February 1939
Earth	Rabbit	19 February 1939 to 7 February 1940
Metal	Dragon	8 February 1940 to 26 January 1941
Metal	Snake	27 January 1941 to 14 February 1942
Water	Horse	15 February 1942 to 4 February 1943
Water	Sheep	5 February 1943 to 24 January 1944
Wood	Monkey	25 January 1944 to 12 February 1945
Wood	Rooster	13 February 1945 to 1 February 1946
Fire	Dog	2 February 1946 to 21 January 1947

Element	Sign	Time Period
Fire	Boar	22 January 1947 to 9 February 1948
Earth	Rat	10 February 1948 to 28 January 1949
Earth	Ox	29 January 1949 to 16 February 1950
Metal	Tiger	17 February 1950 to 5 February 1951
Metal	Rabbit	6 February 1951 to 26 January 1952
Water	Dragon	27 January 1952 to 13 February 1953
Water	Snake	14 February 1953 to 2 February 1954
Wood	Horse	3 February 1954 to 23 January 1955
Wood	Sheep	24 January 1955 to 11 February 1956
Fire	Monkey	12 February 1956 to 30 January 1957
Fire	Rooster	31 January 1957 to 17 February 1958
Earth	Dog	18 February 1958 to 7 February 1959
Earth	Boar	8 February 1959 to 27 January 1960
Metal	Rat	28 January 1960 to 14 February 1961
Metal	Ox	15 February 1961 to 4 February 1962
Water	Tiger	5 February 1962 to 24 January 1963
Water	Rabbit	25 January 1963 to 12 February 1964
Wood	Dragon	13 February 1964 to 1 February 1965
Wood	Snake	2 February 1965 to 20 January 1966
Fire	Horse	21 January 1966 to 8 February 1967
Fire	Sheep	9 February 1967 to 29 January 1968
Earth	Monkey	30 January 1968 to 16 February 1969
Earth	Rooster	17 February 1969 to 5 February 1970
Metal	Dog	6 February 1970 to 26 January 1971
Metal	Boar	27 January 1971 to 15 January 1972
Water	Rat	16 January 1972 to 2 February 1973
Water	Ox	3 February 1973 to 22 January 1974
Wood	Tiger	23 January 1974 to 10 February 1975

Element	Sign	Time Period
Wood	Rabbit	11 February 1975 to 30 January 1976
Fire	Dragon	31 January 1976 to 17 February 1977
Fire	Snake	18 February 1977 to 6 February 1978
Earth	Horse	7 February 1978 to 27 January 1979
Earth	Sheep	28 January 1979 to 15 February 1980
Metal	Monkey	16 February 1980 to 4 February 1981
Metal	Rooster	5 February 1981 to 24 January 1982
Water	Dog	25 January 1982 to 12 February 1983
Water	Boar	13 February 1983 to 1 February 1984
Wood	Rat	2 February 1984 to 19 February 1985
Wood	Ox	20 February 1985 to 8 February 1986
Fire	Tiger	9 February 1986 to 28 January 1987
Fire	Rabbit	29 January 1987 to 16 February 1988
Earth	Dragon	17 February 1988 to 5 February 1989
Earth	Snake	6 February 1989 to 26 January 1990
Metal	Horse	27 January 1990 to 14 February 1991
Metal	Sheep	15 February 1991 to 3 February 1992
Water	Monkey	4 February 1992 to 22 January 1993
Water	Rooster	23 January 1993 to 9 February 1994
Wood	Dog	10 February 1994 to 30 January 1995
Wood	Boar	31 January 1995 to 18 February 1996
Fire	Rat	19 February 1996 to 6 February 1997
Fire	Ox	7 February 1997 to 27 January 1998
Earth	Tiger	28 January 1998 to 15 February 1999
Earth	Rabbit	16 February 1999 to 4 February 2000
Metal	Dragon	5 February 2000 to 23 January 2001
Metal	Snake	24 January 2001 to 11 February 2002
Water	Horse	12 February 2002 to 31 January 2003

Element	Sign	Time Period
Water	Sheep	1 February 2003 to 21 January 2004
Wood	Monkey	22 January 2004 to 8 February 2005
Wood	Rooster	9 February 2005 to 28 January 2006
Fire	Dog	29 January 2006 to 17 February 2007
Fire	Boar	18 February 2007 to 6 February 2008

Magical Alphabets

These examples of magical alphabets are from *Write Your Own Magic* by Richard Webster (Llewellyn, 2001).

Theban

A	B	C	D	E	F	G	H

I	J	K	L	M	N	O	P

Q	R	S	T	U	V	W	X

Y	Z	&

Etruscan

A	B	C	D	E	F	G	H	I	J
Я	Ɔ	ʒ	R	Ǝ	8	D	ㄱ	↖	

K	L	M	N	O	P	Q	R	S	T
ㄣ	⅃	M	Ͷ	◇	H		Δ	⅂	↗

U	V	W	X	Y	Z	CH	IL
	V		X		Z	ʏ	Ƴ

Templar

A	B	C	D	E	F	G	H	I	J
∨	⟨	∧	⟩	◺	◿	△	▽	◇	

K	L	M	N	O	P	Q	R	S	T
◇	◇	◇	✕	∨̇	⟨̇	∧̇	⟩̇	▽̇	◁

U	V	W	X	Y	Z
△̇	◈	◈	◈	∨

The Planetary Hours

Daylight Hours

	Sun	Mon	Tues	Wed	Thurs	Fri	Sat
1	Sun	Moon	Mars	Mercury	Jupiter	Venus	Saturn
2	Venus	Saturn	Sun	Moon	Mars	Mercury	Jupiter
3	Mercury	Jupiter	Venus	Saturn	Sun	Moon	Mars
4	Moon	Mars	Mercury	Jupiter	Venus	Saturn	Sun
5	Saturn	Sun	Moon	Mars	Mercury	Jupiter	Venus
6	Jupiter	Venus	Saturn	Sun	Moon	Mars	Mercury
7	Mars	Mercury	Jupiter	Venus	Saturn	Sun	Moon
8	Sun	Moon	Mars	Mercury	Jupiter	Venus	Saturn
9	Venus	Saturn	Sun	Moon	Mars	Mercury	Jupiter
10	Mercury	Jupiter	Venus	Saturn	Sun	Moon	Mars
11	Moon	Mars	Mercury	Jupiter	Venus	Saturn	Sun
12	Saturn	Sun	Moon	Mars	Mercury	Jupiter	Venus

Nighttime Hours

	Sun	Mon	Tues	Wed	Thurs	Fri	Sat
1	Jupiter	Venus	Saturn	Sun	Moon	Mars	Mercury
2	Mars	Mercury	Jupiter	Venus	Saturn	Sun	Moon
3	Sun	Moon	Mars	Mercury	Jupiter	Venus	Saturn
4	Venus	Saturn	Sun	Moon	Mars	Mercury	Jupiter
5	Mercury	Jupiter	Venus	Saturn	Sun	Moon	Mars
6	Moon	Mars	Mercury	Jupiter	Venus	Saturn	Sun
7	Saturn	Sun	Moon	Mars	Mercury	Jupiter	Venus
8	Jupiter	Venus	Saturn	Sun	Moon	Mars	Mercury
9	Mars	Mercury	Jupiter	Venus	Saturn	Sun	Moon
10	Sun	Moon	Mars	Mercury	Jupiter	Venus	Saturn
11	Venus	Saturn	Sun	Moon	Mars	Mercury	Jupiter
12	Mercury	Jupiter	Venus	Saturn	Sun	Moon	Mars

Notes

Introduction

1. Reverend Ray T. Malbrough, *The Magical Power of the Saints: Evocations and Candle Rituals* (St. Paul, MN: Llewellyn Publications, 1998), 68.

2. *Encyclopaedia Britannica,* Micropaedia, Volume II (Chicago, IL: Encyclopaedia Britannica, Inc., Fifteenth edition, 1983), 506.

3. *Encyclopaedia Britannica,* Macropaedia, Volume 4 (Chicago, IL: Encyclopaedia Britannica, Inc., Fifteenth edition, 1983), 744.

4. Gordon Grimley, *The Origins of Everything* (St. Albans, UK: Mayflower Books, 1973), 67.

5. Barbara G. Walker, *A Women's Encyclopedia of Myths and Secrets* (San Francisco, CA: Harper and Row, Inc., 1983), 134–135.

Chapter One

1. Aleister Crowley, *Magick Liber ABA*, Book 4 (Originally published in 1913. Reprinted by: York Beach, ME: Samuel Weiser, Inc., 1994), 126.

2. Florence Farr, quoted in Mary K. Greer, *Women of the Golden Dawn: Rebels and Priestesses* (Rochester, VT: Park Street Press, 1995), 64.

3. Pheylonian Beeswax Candles, Box 56, Marlbank, Ontario, Canada. Their website is: http://www.philoxia.com.

4. Doreen Valiente, *Natural Magic* (Custer, WA: Phoenix Publishing Inc., 1975), 21.

Chapter Two

1. Bill Harris, *The Good Luck Book* (Owings Mills, MD: Oppenheimer Publishers, Inc., 1996), 32.

Chapter Three

1. C. A. S. Williams, *Outlines of Chinese Symbolism and Art Motives*, 3rd revised edition (Shanghai, China: Kelly and Walsh Limited, 1941), 182. (Originally published as *Outlines of Chinese Symbolism* by Customs College Press, Peiping, China, 1931.)

2. Leonardo da Vinci, quoted in Margaret Noëlle Leven, *The Cosmic Rainbow* (Willagee, Australia: Margaret Leven, 2000), 43.

3. Roland Hunt, *The Seven Keys to Colour Healing* (London, UK: The C. W. Daniel Company Limited, 1971), 103–104.

4. Martin Lang, *Character Analysis through Color* (Westport, CT: The Crimson Press, 1940), 61.

Chapter Four

1. M. Luckiesh, *Language of Colour* (New York, Dodd, Mead and Company, 1918).

2. Carl G. Jung, *Memories, Dreams, Reflections*, recorded and edited by Aniela Jaffe (London, UK: Collins and Routledge and Kegan Paul, 1963), 308.

Chapter Six

1. Ken Ring, *Predicting the Weather by the Moon* (Christchurch, NZ: Hazard Press, 2000).

2. Zolar, *Zolar's Magick of Color* (New York, NY: Simon and Schuster, Inc., 1994), 123.

3. Grand Orient (pseudonym of Arthur Edward Waite), *Complete Manual of Occult Divination*, Volume 1 (New Hyde Park, NY: University Books, Inc., 1972), 208.

Chapter Seven

1. Michael Howard, *Incense and Candle Burning* (London, UK: The Aquarian Press, 1991), 97.

2. Leo Vinci, *Incense: Its Ritual Significance, Use and Preparation* (New York, NY: Samuel Weiser, Inc., 1980), 19.

3. Francis Barrett, *The Magus* (London: Lackington, Allen, and Co., 1801), 93. Many editions of this book are available. Mine is a facsimile edition, published by The Aquarian Press, Wellingborough, England, in 1989.

Chapter Ten

1. Nigel Pennick, *The Secret Lore of Runes and Other Ancient Alphabets* (London, UK: Rider and Company, 1991), 177–181.

2. Paul Christian, *Histoire de la Magie*, 1870.

3. Cornelius Agrippa, *Three Books of Occult Philosophy*, Donald Tyson, editor (St. Paul, MN: Llewellyn Publications, 1993), 560–562.

4. Forty-six alphabets are shown in *Encyclopaedia of the Occult, Paranormal and Magick Practices* by Brian Lane (London, UK: Warner Books, 1996), 16–19. 23 alphabets are shown in *The Magician's Companion* by Bill Whitcomb (St. Paul, MN: Llewellyn Publications, 1993), 361–398.

5. Bill Whitcomb, *The Magician's Reflection* (St. Paul, MN: Llewellyn Publications, 1999), 189–195.

Chapter Thirteen

1. Max Maven, *Max Maven's Book of Fortunetelling* (New York, NY: Prentice Hall, 1992), 175.

Chapter Fourteen

1. Richard Webster, *Practical Guide to Past-Life Memories* (St. Paul, MN: Llewellyn Publications, 2001).

2. Mark Forstater, *The Spiritual Teaching of Marcus Aurelius* (London, UK: Hodder and Stoughton, 2000), 91.

Suggested Reading

Agrippa, Cornelius. *Three Books of Occult Philosophy*. Donald Tyson, editor. St. Paul, MN: Llewellyn Publications, 1993.

Argüelles, José and Miriam. *Mandala*. Boston, Mass: Shambhala Publications, Inc., 1972.

Barrett, Francis. *The Magus*. London, UK: Lackington, Allen, and Co., 1801.

Buckland, Raymond. *Practical Candleburning Rituals*. St. Paul, MN: Llewellyn Publications, 1970.

———. *Advanced Candle Magick*. St. Paul, MN: Llewellyn Publications, 1996.

Crowley, Aleister. *Magick Liber ABA*, Book 4 (Originally published in 1913). Reprinted by: York Beach, ME: Samuel Weiser, Inc., 1994.

Dahlke, Rudiger. *Mandalas of the World*. New York, NY: Sterling Publishing Co., Inc., 1992.

DeJong, Lana. *Candlefire*. Cottonwood, AZ: Esoteric Publications, 1973.

Dey, Charmaine. *The Magic Candle*. Las Vegas, NV: Bell, Book and Candle, 1979.

Dunwich, Gerina. *Wicca Candle Magick*. Secaucus, NJ: Citadel Press, 1997.

Forstater, Mark. *The Spiritual Teaching of Marcus Aurelius*. London, UK: Hodder and Stoughton, 2000.

Greer, Mary K. *Women of the Golden Dawn: Rebels and Priestesses*. Rochester, VT: Park Street Press, 1995.

Grimley, Gordon. *The Origins of Everything*. St. Albans, UK: Mayflower Books, 1973.

Harris, Bill. *The Good Luck Book*. Owings Mills, MD: Oppenheimer Publishers, Inc., 1996.

Hodson, Geoffrey. *Lecture Notes: The School of Wisdom,* Volume 1. Adyar, India: The Theosophical Publishing House, 1955.

Howard, Michael. *Incense and Candle Burning*. London, UK: The Aquarian Press, 1991.

Hunt, Roland. *The Seven Keys to Colour Healing*. London, UK: The C. W. Daniel Company Limited, 1971.

Ketch, Tina. *Candle Lighting Encyclopedia*. Stone Mountain, GA: Tina Ketch, 1991.

Lane, Brian. *Encyclopaedia of the Occult, Paranormal and Magick Practices*. London, UK: Warner Books, 1996.

Lang, Martin. *Character Analysis through Color.* Westport, CT: The Crimson Press, 1940.

Leven, Margaret Noëlle. *The Cosmic Rainbow.* Willagee, Australia: Margaret Leven, 2000.

Malbrough, Reverend Ray T. *The Magical Power of the Saints: Evocations and Candle Rituals*. St. Paul, MN: Llewellyn Publications, 1998.

Maven, Max. *Max Maven's Book of Fortunetelling*. New York, NY: Prentice Hall, 1992.

Morrish, Furze. *Outline of Astro-Psychology*. London, UK: Rider and Company, 1952.

Pajeon, Kala and Ketz. *The Candle Magick Workbook*. Secaucus, NJ: Citadel Press, 1991.

Pennick, Nigel. *The Secret Lore of Runes and Other Ancient Alphabets*. London, UK: Rider and Company, 1991.

Smith, Steven R. *Wylundt's Book of Incense*. York Beach, ME: Samuel Weiser, Inc., 1989.

Valiente, Doreen. *Natural Magic*. Custer, WA: Phoenix Publishing Inc., 1975.

Vinci, Leo. *Incense: Its Ritual Significance, Use and Preparation*. New York, NY: Samuel Weiser, Inc., 1980.

Walker, Barbara G. *A Women's Encyclopedia of Myths and Secrets*. San Francisco, CA: Harper and Row, Inc., 1983.

Webster, Richard. *Feng Shui for Beginners*. St. Paul, MN: Llewellyn Publications, 1997.

———. *Practical Guide to Past-Life Memories*. St. Paul, MN: Llewellyn Publications, 2001.

———. *Pendulum Magic for Beginners*. St. Paul, MN: Llewellyn Publications, 2002.

Whitaker, Charlene. *Candles, Meditation and Healing*. St. Paul, MN: Llewellyn Publications, 2000.

Whitcomb, Bill. *The Magician's Companion*. St. Paul, MN: Llewellyn Publications, 1993.

———. *The Magician's Reflection*. St. Paul, MN: Llewellyn Publications, 1999.

Williams, C. A. S. *Outlines of Chinese Symbolism and Art Motives*. 3rd revised edition. Shanghai, China: Kelly and Walsh Limited, 1941.

Index

To Write to the Author

If you wish to contact the author or would like more information about this book, please write to the author in care of Llewellyn Worldwide and we will forward your request. Both the author and publisher appreciate hearing from you and learning of your enjoyment of this book and how it has helped you. Llewellyn Worldwide cannot guarantee that every letter written to the author can be answered, but all will be forwarded. Please write to:

Richard Webster

℅ Llewellyn Worldwide

P.O. Box 64383, Dept. 0-7387-0535-7

St. Paul, MN 55164-0383, U.S.A.

Please enclose a self-addressed stamped envelope for reply, or $1.00 to cover costs. If outside U.S.A., enclose international postal reply coupon.

Many of Llewellyn's authors have websites with additional informa-tion and resources. For more information, please visit our website at http://www.llewellyn.com.

Read unique articles by Llewellyn authors, recommendations by experts, and information on new releases. To receive a **free** copy of Llewellyn's consumer magazine, *New Worlds of Mind & Spirit,* simply call 1-877-NEW-WRLD or visit our website at www.llewellyn.com and click on *New Worlds.*

☽ LLEWELLYN ORDERING INFORMATION

Order Online:
Visit our website at www.llewellyn.com, select your books, and order them on our secure server.

Order by Phone:
- Call toll-free within the U.S. at 1-877-NEW-WRLD (1-877-639-9753). Call toll-free within Canada at 1-866-NEW-WRLD (1-866-639-9753)
- We accept VISA, MasterCard, and American Express

Order by Mail:
Send the full price of your order (MN residents add 7% sales tax) in U.S. funds, plus postage & handling to:

Llewellyn Worldwide
P.O. Box 64383, Dept. 0-7387-0535-7
St. Paul, MN 55164-0383, U.S.A.

Postage & Handling:

Standard (U.S., Mexico, & Canada). If your order is:
$49.99 and under, add $3.00
$50.00 and over, FREE STANDARD SHIPPING

AK, HI, PR: $15.00 for one book plus $1.00 for each additional book.

International Orders (airmail only):
$16.00 for one book plus $3.00 for each additional book

Orders are processed within 2 business days.
Please allow for normal shipping time. Postage and handling rates subject to change.

DOWSING FOR BEGINNERS

The Art of Discovering: Water, Treasure, Gold, Oil, Artifacts

Richard Webster

This book provides everything you need to know to become a successful dowser. Dowsing is the process of using a dowsing rod or pendulum to divine for anything you wish to locate: water, oil, gold, ancient ruins, lost objects, or even missing people. Dowsing can also be used to determine if something is safe to eat or drink, or to diagnose and treat allergies and diseases.

Learn about the tools you'll use: angle and divining rods, pendulums, wands—even your own hands and body can be used as dowsing tools! Explore basic and advanced dowsing techniques, beginning with methods for dowsing the terrain for water. Find how to dowse anywhere in the world without leaving your living room, with the technique of map dowsing. Discover the secrets of dowsing to determine optimum planting locations; to monitor your pets' health and well-being; to detect harmful radiation in your environment; to diagnose disease; to determine psychic potential; to locate archeological remains; to gain insight into yourself, and more! *Dowsing for Beginners* is a complete "how-to-do-it" guide to learning an invaluable skill.

1-56718-802-8, 256 pp., 5¼ x 8, illus., photos $9.95

PALM READING FOR BEGINNERS
Find the Future in the Palm of Your Hand
Richard Webster

Announce in any gathering that you read palms and you will be flocked by people thrilled to show you their hands. When you are have finished *Palm Reading for Beginners*, you will be able to look at anyone's palm (including your own) and confidently and effectively tell them about their personality, love life, hidden talents, career options, prosperity, and health.

Palmistry is possibly the oldest of the occult sciences, with basic principles that have not changed in 2,600 years. This step-by-step guide clearly explains the basics, as well as advanced research conducted in the past few years on such subjects as dermatoglyphics.

1-56718-791-9, 264 pp., 5³⁄₁₆ x 8, illus. **$9.95**

PENDULUM MAGIC FOR BEGINNERS

Power to Achieve All Goals

Richard Webster

The pendulum is a simple, accurate, and versatile device consisting of a weight attached to a chain or thread. Arguably the most underrated item in the magician's arsenal, the pendulum can reveal information not found any other way. It can read energy patterns, extracting information from deep inside our subconscious.

This book will teach you how to perform apparent miracles such as finding lost objects, helping your potted plants grow better, protecting yourself from harmful foods, detecting dishonesty in others, and even choosing the right neighborhood. Explore past lives, recall dreams, release blocks to achieving happiness, and send your wishes out into the universe.

0-7387-0192-0, 288 pp., 5³⁄₁₆ x 8, illus. $12.95